GAIL DUFF has been a writer, broadcaster, speech therapist, singer, song-writer, dancer, folk animateur and community arts worker. For as long as she can remember, the seasons and traditions of the year have been an important focus of her life. She feels that she was born a Pagan and has been a practising Wiccan for over eight years. She has successfully resurrected some of the folk traditions of south-east England and regularly takes part in many more. *The Wheel of the Wiccan Year* draws upon many of these authentic practices, and also includes traditional songs and ancient lore.

THE WHEEL OF THE WICCAN YEAR

How to Enrich Your Life through the Magic of the Seasons

GAIL DUFF

LONDON · SYDNEY · AUCKLAND · JOHANNESBURG

3 5 7 9 10 8 6 4 2

First published in 2002 by Rider,
an imprint of Ebury Press, Random House,
20 Vauxhall Bridge Road, London SW1V 2SA

Random House Australia (Pty) Limited
20 Alfred Street, Milsons Point, Sydney,
New South Wales 2061, Australia

Random House New Zealand Limited
18 Poland Road, Glenfield,
Auckland 10, New Zealand

Random House South Africa (Pty) Limited
Endulini, 5A Jubilee Road,
Parktown 2193, South Africa

The Random House Group Limited Reg. No. 954009

Papers used by Rider are natural, recyclable products made from wood grown
in sustainable forests.

Illustrations by Deborah Robinson

Printed and bound by Mackay's of Chatham plc, Kent

A CIP catalogue record for this book
is available from the British Library

ISBN 0-7126-1230-0

CONTENTS

Acknowledgements

A great big thank you to Debbie Robinson, not only for the wonderful illustrations but for encouraging me along the way, and to her husband David for reading the manuscript and pointing out my occasionally crazy grammar and spelling!

*For Rabble and friends with whom
I share the riches of the Wheel of the Year,
and for Wolf, who started it all.*

INTRODUCTION

BEFORE YOU BEGIN

The cycle of light and dark, of planting and harvest, of leaves budding, opening and falling, is an ever-turning wheel that has no beginning and no end. It rolls through the seasons, changing the landscape, and influencing the things that we do and the way that we feel. Each time of the year is special, with its own particular feelings, smells and atmospheres – and, if we allow it, its effect on our lives.

The religion or philosophy of Wicca works with this wheel; the Wiccan year is divided by eight festivals that relate to what is happening in the natural world around us. The festivals tell the story of the Goddess and God and they also act as guides to our spiritual progress. Each one leads into another and has its own unique joys.

These festivals can be marked in as big or as small a way as you wish. You can celebrate on your own, with a few friends or with a large gathering, and what you do is up to you. At Samhain, for example, you can make a pumpkin lantern, write a ritual, cook special food, make incense and decorate the house, or you can simply lay an autumn leaf on a shelf and reflect for a few minutes on how some parts of your life are reaching fulfilment and how some parts need to be left behind.

There are many books of Wiccan rituals. Wiccans all share the same basic beliefs and attitudes, but each individual has their own way of expressing things and doing things. What I have tried to do in this book is to share my pleasures and experiences gained by travelling the wheel. I hope it will help to convey the meaning of the festivals to those who may be just beginning on the Wiccan path, and will also provide the means to enrich them through songs, plays, meditations and the smaller details such as incense or special food.

Enjoy it; use it to help your understanding of the Wheel of Life and to bring you closer to the Goddess and God. However, before you begin to celebrate the festivals, there are certain things you will need to think about, items to acquire and facts to know.

WICCA

The ancestors of Wicca are the old Pagan religions, which were practised in harmony with the phases of the Moon and with the seasons of the year. These two aspects still play a significant part in the way that we work and celebrate. The name comes from an Anglo-Saxon word meaning 'wise' and hence you get other names for it such as the Craft of the Wise or the Way of the Wise, sometimes shortened to 'the Way' or 'the Craft'. It was once pronounced *witch-a* (female version) and *witch-e* (male), and so practitioners became known as witches. They were, and often still are, teachers, healers and helpers in times of trouble. Any other connotations to the word are the result of two thousand years of bad press!

What happened to the Old Religion during the times of persecution, no one can really say. What we do know is that Gerald Gardner, who belonged to a coven (the name for a group of witches) in the British New Forest, together with other members such as Doreen Valiente, produced a 'Book of Shadows' (see below) containing the words for the seasonal rituals and other rites. His branch of Wicca was called 'Gardnerian' Wicca and was the first to be made known after the repeal of the Witchcraft Act in 1951. In the 1960s, these words and ceremonies were adapted by Alex Sanders, whose branch of Wicca

became known as 'Alexandrian'. Since then, interest has grown rapidly and there are now many branches of Wicca, many covens and also many solitary practitioners. Although there are differences between them in terms of practice, they all hold the same basic beliefs.

Wicca is still a nature-based religion. It works with the seasons of the year and the paths of the Sun and Moon. Its festivals coincide with the old agricultural festivals and its practitioners aim to organise their lives around the Wheel of the Year. Because Wicca is nature-based, its practitioners think about the natural world, and strive to care for it in as many ways as possible.

Most Wiccans believe that there is one life force or creator, which is beyond our human comprehension. We seek to understand this in ways that we find easy to imagine, and think in terms of two opposite deities, the Goddess and the God. Where other religions are strictly patriarchal, Wiccans believe that you cannot have a male principle without a female principle. We also believe that there is a part of the Goddess and God within everybody and that we should each strive to balance the male and female aspects of ourselves.

Because of this belief in two deities, men and women are equally respected and we recognise and admire the differences between us. We regard sex as something joyful and sacred, a gift from the deities, and nothing to be ashamed of so long as it is between loving partners.

One of the other main differences between Wicca and other religions is that there is no central hierarchy. Most formal covens are run by a High Priest and High Priestess, but every member of the Craft is a Priest or Priestess, and you can just as easily work alone or come together for festivals with other like-minded people without there being a formal leader. You can choose exactly how you celebrate and what you do.

There is only one rule in Wicca: 'An it harm none, do what thou wilt.' This is all you need. It means that we strive to be true to ourselves while harming nothing, including ourselves. It takes in every other law that has ever been written and needs a lot of thought and care to live

by. One other point that has ensured that Wiccans try to act always for good is the belief that whatever you do comes back to you threefold, either in this life or the next.

Wiccans believe in reincarnation and that we come into the world with specific lessons to learn. If they are not learned in this life, then we may have to come back and face them again. Have you ever felt that similar problems keep recurring in your life? This is probably because dealing with them involves a shift of opinion or a move away from old habits. If you do not do this the first time, then a similar opportunity will come up until you take responsibility for doing something about it.

Wiccans usually regularly set themselves goals for learning lessons and for self-improvement; these lessons and tasks are often set within the Wheel of the Year. They could be improvements in the way that we handle situations or react to other people, or other more obvious ones like learning a new skill, giving up smoking or other bad habits, or being more disciplined in the way we organise ourselves. Everyone has something different that they would like to achieve each year.

Healing has always been one of the tasks of the witch and this is now becoming easier again with the availability of courses on anything from herbal medicine to Indian head massage. Divination is another skill that many Wiccans like to practise, whether with runes and tarot cards or by staring into the fire, a dark mirror or running water. It is used more as a guide to self-knowledge and meditation rather than foretelling the future.

Do Wiccans work magic? Yes, we do. Magic is simply the power of thought and concentration. If you want and need something to happen and believe that it will, then you will probably be successful. However, you must be sure of what it is that you want and you must never harm anyone or manipulate anyone through your magic (that includes trying to make a named person fall in love with you!). Rhymes, chants, candle-burning or any other actions that help concentrate your thoughts are your 'spells'.

Wicca is first and foremost a joyful, loving and caring religion and those who practise it take every opportunity to celebrate the fact.

THE GODDESS AND GOD

The Goddess and God are always with us and their story is played out within the Wheel of the Year. Over thousands of years their different aspects have been turned into a myriad other deities, all of which are parts of the one. So Aphrodite, Goddess of Love, and Hecate, Goddess of the Underworld, both represent parts of the one Goddess, who is both Goddess of Love and of Death and of every other part of our lives.

The Goddess is linked with the Moon and its phases of waxing, full and waning. She is often referred to as the Triple Goddess who is three in one, Maiden, Mother and Crone, with all the attributes and qualities that each one possesses. She is also Goddess of the Earth and of the stars, of creativity and inspiration and, in the story of the year, she is both Mother and Lover to the God.

The God is Lord of Life and Death, of day and night, of woods and wild places, of laughter and freedom. He is associated with the ancient God of the Hunt and so, like Pan, he is often seen as having horns. Every year, he is born with the new light at Yule and lays down his life for the harvest.

THE ELEMENTS

It has long been recognised that our lives are made up of different interwoven aspects. We have a physical body, we are able to think, we have passions and causes and we have emotions. We also have a spirit that is our very essence. These aspects not only apply to people but to the whole of the Earth and what is on it. They are governed by the Elements of Earth (physical), Air (thought), Fire (passions), Water (emotions) and Spirit. Wiccans believe that each Element has its own Guardian Spirits and we can call upon these Spirits to guard our circle (see page 18) and to help us in the work that we do. Each Element is connected with a different direction, hence the marking of the quarters in the circle. Earth is in the North, Air is East, Fire is South and Water is West. Spirit is contained within the centre of the circle.

THE WHEEL OF THE YEAR

Eight festivals divide the Wiccan Wheel of the Year. They are connected to the seasons and the farming calendar and also to the story of the Goddess and God. These festivals are called Sabbats, from the Greek *sabatu*, which means 'to rest'. They were once holy days (or holidays), when work briefly ceased and everyone celebrated. They are about six weeks apart and they occur at times of significant change, either in the position of the sun or in weather patterns.

The original Celtic peoples celebrated only four of the festivals. These were the ones which marked significant changes in the agricultural year that governed their lives. Today, these festivals are called the Greater Sabbats, and their dates are fixed. Originally, they were probably movable (although at the same time of the year) and celebrated when the weather and the crops and possibly other circumstances were right. In the farming calendar of later centuries they became known as the 'cross-quarter days' which fall between the Solstices and Equinoxes. They are Samhain (31 October), Imbolc (2 February), Beltane (1 May) and Lughnasadh or Lammas (1 August).

The Lesser Sabbats are the Solstices and Equinoxes, which occur between the cross-quarter days. They were celebrated in Megalithic times, hence the stone circles, and later by Greeks, Romans and Norse peoples. The Solstices are the two points when the Sun is closest to the Earth and highest in the sky (Summer Solstice) and when it is furthest

away and lowest (Winter Solstice). After these days, there is change as the Sun alters course. The Equinoxes are the days when the hours of dark and light are equal, after which, although the Sun continues to move in the same direction, we progress from dark to light or light to dark. The order of the Wheel of the Year is therefore:

- Samhain: 31 October
- Yule, the Winter Solstice: on or around 21 December
- Imbolc: 2 February
- Ostara, the Spring Equinox, on or around 21 March
- Beltane: 1 May
- Litha, the Summer Solstice: on or around 21 June
- Lammas or Lughnasadh: 1 August
- Mabon, the Autumn Equinox: on or around 21 September.

Every change in the Sun's relationship to the Earth, in the quality of light, in the weather or the pattern of growing has a profound relationship to the way we act and feel. Celebrating the festivals and observing the changes in the year put us in touch with the natural world and helps us to relate it to the changes within our hearts and lives. We are all on a spiritual journey and we all have our tasks to do in this life and our lessons to learn. Working within the Wheel of the Year will help us go from stage to stage at the right pace.

Throughout the book, I have used the metaphor of the seed and the harvest to represent the projects that we undertake within the year. We identify our seeds, name them and plant them, nurture them through the summer and finally harvest them. We take stock of the harvest and then have a break before beginning other quests next year.

Punctuating the year with a celebration every six weeks, rather than the one annual binge of Christmas, also helps to keep your life in balance and, just as importantly, ensures that you always have an occasion to work towards, to look forward to and to enjoy.

Folk traditions

In each description of a festival, you will also find some information about the folk traditions and customs that also take place at that particular time of the year. I have done this because they are an integral part of my own life and I base many of my practices on the wider folk calendar. Their roots go way back to before anything was written down so nobody can be sure of their origins. Some people believe that folk traditions and Paganism are inextricably linked, and others believe just as strongly that they are not. Some Pagans misinterpret folk customs and some who take part in folk customs would hotly deny Pagan links. To those of us who are committed to one or both of these ways of life, it should not matter. What we take from these customs now and what we make of them are up to us. They are 'folk' customs and that means they belong to us all. I have chosen to weave them together because it feels right for who I am and what I do. From my point of view, the Pagan Wheel of the Year and the calendar customs enrich each other. However, we must respect each other's views and not let differences tear our traditions apart. The world is big enough for us all.

Working alone or in a group

Everything in this book has been written so that you can celebrate the festivals alone, with one other person or in a group. I always work in a group at these main festivals and so the wording is slightly biased in that direction. If you are working alone, just go through the text before you begin and change 'we' to 'I', and so on.

Each way has its own advantages. When working alone you can concentrate more and stop and meditate whenever you wish. The whole thing is far more personal and probably more serious. In a group, there is the joy of shared experience and ideas.

If you are just setting out, choose the members of your group very carefully and keep things small at first, maybe with just three or four people. Don't actively go out and seek people to join you. You will

probably find that the right people are those who are already close to you. Never just ask people round for 'a good night out'. Make what you are going to do very plain and discuss it with your intended guests beforehand. Your friends may have very different ideas and you may find you are going against their religious beliefs. Although shared festivals are fun, their intention is serious and should never be regarded as 'good for a laugh' or 'something different to do on a Saturday night'.

USING THIS BOOK

A wheel has no beginning and no end, so you can embark upon the journey of the Wheel of the Year at any time. Even if you have not 'planted your seeds' in the spring, you can still look back over the year at harvest time to see what you have achieved. If you begin at Samhain, treat the next few weeks as preparation. If you begin at Midsummer, count your blessings before you set out. The spiritual journey is always there and you can begin it at any time.

Each seasonal festival has been given a separate chapter. Within each chapter is a 'Things to do' section. After reading it through, you can choose which rituals, visualisations, songs or plays are suitable for you at this time. You may simply wish to read through the words, you may want to try one or two things or you may have the will and the time for them all. It is entirely up to you. At the end of the section is a 'Complete ritual', which incorporates most of the suggestions in an order that I think makes sense. I have deliberately done this so as not to lay down a rigid structure. From this, you can write your own personal ritual, using the words and suggestions given, making it the right length and with the right items for your own celebrations. Rather than leafing backwards and forwards through the book at the time of your ritual, copy everything that you want to do beforehand into your Book of Shadows (see page 10) in the right order. You will then have a permanent record of what you have done and you can build on it or alter it next year if you wish.

On reading through the book, I realised that there seemed to be a lot of 'clearing out the old' activities but, when you think about it, we clear rubbish from our houses every week. There is no reason why, as we grow and change, the spiritual or emotional rubbish should not go out too. This is just one of the things that you can choose to do or not.

If something doesn't quite work for you or if you can think of words that you prefer more, then change it. I change mine very slightly every year. The words in the following pages are simply what I used in the particular year that I was writing this book. What mustn't change, though, is the theme of any particular festival. You can't 're-invent the wheel', but the words used to tell the story can be changed. In this way, the basic rituals will become more and more personal to you and to the people with whom you celebrate.

THE ORIGINAL BOOK OF SHADOWS

The original Book of Shadows, on which most Wiccan rituals are still based, was written by Gerald Gardner, with considerable input from the late Doreen Valiente, mostly in the 1950s. In it were all the Wiccan rituals as he practised them at the time, including celebrations for the different festivals of the year, rituals for full Moons and for rites of passage (birth, marriage, and so on). It was a tradition that every initiate into the Craft copied out his own Book of Shadows by hand from that belonging to the High Priest or Priestess of the coven and then added to it as they wished over the years. Mine came from my teacher who was in an Alexandrian coven (founded by Alex Sanders in the 1960s) and, no matter how many other books I have read over the years, I always return to it. Like the folk singer, I need to hear or read the original song and develop from that, rather than developing a modern version. In this way, I stay close to the tradition and maintain its themes and ideas but am still able to incorporate my own writing.

The rituals in this original Book of Shadows are very beautiful but very short and have been built on by many people who have practised them in many different ways. Janet and Stewart Farrar, in their books *Eight Sabbats for Witches* and *The Witches' Way* (printed together as *The Witches' Bible*), give many of these original words.

YOUR OWN BOOK OF SHADOWS

The Book of Shadows today has become something more like your own personal Wiccan diary. You will need a hard-backed notebook, no smaller than A4 and with plain paper. Or, if handwriting really isn't your thing, you can use a computer, plain computer paper and a loose-leaf binder into which you can also put drawings and hand-written notes. Black used to be the recommended colour but it is best to choose a colour that you really like.

This will become your diary, notebook and handbook of rituals. You can begin by writing out your seasonal rituals. After the ritual, make notes on how it went. This book also contains projects that specifically make use of writing or drawing in your Book of Shadows. There are also meditations and visualisations which need to be recorded. You can also use it to write up your dreams or record what you have seen or what makes an impression on you during a walk in the countryside. Eventually it will become a detailed account of your thoughts, feelings, successes and lessons as you go through the year. Through it you will be able to chart your changes and progression. Once it becomes a habit, you will never be able to do without it.

RHYMING

It has often been said that affirmations, chants and spells are more powerful if they are said in rhyme. Certainly, when you are 'ad libbing' on your own, trying to find rhymes helps you to concentrate, and the more you do it the easier it becomes. The rituals in this book are made up of rhymes, chants and blank verse. If you would like to add more rhymes, then by all means do so.

SONGS

The tunes for the songs in this book are all traditional folk tunes with no copyright. If you do not know the tunes, just read the words as poems.

SPECIAL THINGS

There are certain items that you will always need for your seasonal rituals, but although they are special and kept only for use within your circle, you do not have to spend a lot of money on them. Certainly you can buy beautiful craftsman-made items but they are not essential to the success of your ritual. Always bear in mind that everyday items were originally used in the circle. This was mainly to avoid detection in the days when witchcraft was illegal, but also because no one had the money to buy anything else. Below are the basics. You will also need one or two additional things for some of the festivals, so check several days beforehand to make sure that you have everything.

ATHAME

This is the name for the knife that is your working tool. Traditionally, it had to be black-handled, but this is not compulsory. Use it to draw your circle, to invoke the Elements and to bless the wine, and also for things like cutting the cake at Beltane and apples at Samhain, even digging candlewax out of holders or filing down candles so they fit into various shaped containers. Keep it safely in a sheath, in a place where it will not be stolen or used for the wrong purpose. It should never, ever be used as a weapon or a threat. Look on it more as you do your kitchen knives – a useful tool.

WAND

Some people dislike bringing knives or anything made from metal into the circle and prefer to use a wand instead of an athame. This is made from wood and is traditionally as long as your forearm. To find your own wand, simply go out into a wood or into a park where there are a lot of trees, knowing your intention. You will probably find a suitable twig. This is all you need.

INCENSE

This is used to purify the space within your circle and also as an offering to the Spirits of Air. The loose type that is burned on a charcoal disc is the best. You will also need a stand or dish on which to burn it. Ceramic ones are best as they conduct less heat than metal. If you do not wish to make up your own incense, you can buy it ready-made. Highly recommended are those by Starchild (see Resources, page 216).

SALT OR HOLY STONE

A dish of pure sea salt or a stone with a hole in it is used as an offering to the Spirits of Earth. Use any small pottery dish or a large shell for the salt.

WATER DISH

A small dish of water is used as an offering to the Spirits of Water. Use any small pottery dish.

CANDLES AND CANDLESTICKS

A candle in a holder is an offering to the Spirits of Fire. You will also need two matching candlesticks for your altar. It is nice, but not essential, to change the colour of the candles in these holders for each festival. However, ordinary white household candles are cheaper and always available. A candle lantern, that does not get too hot to pick up, is essential when you are working in semi-darkness with a sheet of words to read. It is traditional to mark the four quarters of your circle with candles or with lanterns. Big, sturdy church candles or nightlight lanterns are ideal. At all times, make sure your candles and incense are safe and never leave them burning unattended.

CHALICE

You will need a chalice to hold your wine. It doesn't have to be metal; there are some really attractive pottery ones. Buy to suit your own taste and pocket or have a look in your cupboards to see if you have anything suitable.

PLATE

Keep a special plate for cakes.

CAULDRON

In the old days, a cauldron was not special. It was the cooking vessel that was in every household for use in cooking over an open fire. Mine is an original that was given to me many years ago as a piece of antique cooking equipment. They are made nowadays mainly for the use of people who take part in historical re-enactments, but they do tend to be expensive. A cast iron cooking pot can be used just as well.

TIBETAN BOWL

This is not essential but, if you have one, use it in the circle as an aid to concentration.

DRUM

This is useful for keeping the rhythm of dances and songs but, again, not essential. A tambourine can be used instead.

OTHER USEFUL THINGS TO HAVE IN STORE
- Matches
- Wax tapers

- Candle snuffer
- Garden flares (for working outside)
- Pencils
- Plain paper
- Blu-tack or something similar

PUTTING YOUR HOUSE IN ORDER

If you are celebrating indoors, make sure the space that you are going to work in is clean and tidy and that your house is pleasant for people to enter. This might sound pedantic, but you are aiming to create an enjoyable experience for yourself and others and, more importantly, you are inviting the presence of the Goddess and God and the four Elements into your working space. For a short time, your house will become a temple, so prepare it with reverence. Burning scented oils in the house during the day will create an appropriate atmosphere and vases of flowers or sprigs of greenery add to the sense of occasion. There are suggestions for decorations in each chapter.

OUTSIDE SPACE

If you have a secluded garden, hold your celebrations there. If you choose to go out into the countryside, make sure you find a place where you will not be trespassing and where you will not be disturbed. Be really efficient about taking everything that you need. Light fires only where they will do no damage and leave the place in better order than you find it. That means things like preventing your candlewax from dripping on the ground or onto stones and trees (put candles on foil plates), picking up your own litter and also picking up any litter that is there when you arrive.

ALTAR

You will need a small table that you can use as an altar. Ideally, you will only use it in rituals and bring it out whenever you need to cast a circle. However, this not absolutely essential. If you have special coverings that you only use within your circle you can quickly transform what is normally a coffee table. When you are working in the garden, use wooden garden furniture. If you are in the wilds, a suitable tree stump or log provides a ready-made surface that does not need to be covered.

Set up your altar in the north of the room, or the north side of your circle. Cover it and put a candle at either end. In the centre, arrange the salt, incense, a single candle and a bowl of water, according to the directions of their elements (salt in the North, incense in the East, candle in the South and water in the West). Wear your athame but put your wand on the right of the right-hand candle. At the other end put the chalice of wine and, if there is room, the cakes. If there isn't room, put the cakes underneath, together with any other items (tapers, cauldron, extra candles, pieces of paper, and so on) that are needed for that particular festival. Sometimes it takes quite a time to get everything ready, but it is worth it when a ritual goes smoothly. Don't feel bad if you miss something out and you don't realise until you need it. We've all done it and have had to improvise our way through without the needed item!

LIGHTING

Work by candlelight rather than artificial light. Have candles or lanterns at the four quarters beside your altar candles. If the room still seems dark, place lanterns or nightlights at strategic points.

DRESS

This is a special occasion, so wear something special. In respect for the Goddess and God, have a bath or shower, fix your hair and make yourself look good. Many Wiccans have special clothes for wearing within the circle. These clothes can be robes or simply ordinary clothes used only at these times. Choose natural fibres whenever you can. Other people just put on their best clothes. It is customary to take your shoes off within the circle, out of respect for the Goddess and God and the Elements. Watches should also be left outside because they can set up negative vibrations.

THE CIRCLE OF PROTECTION

When you are working with the Elements and calling upon the Goddess and God to be with you in your celebrations, you must always work within a circle of protection. This keeps out any evil influences that may be lurking about in the ether and also contains and concentrates your powers of thought and projection. The words that I use are loosely adapted from the old Book of Shadows.

When you are ready to begin your ritual, stand at your altar with any other person taking part standing behind you. Ask everyone to be quiet. Face North with your altar in front of you. Hold your athame or wand with two hands and point it slightly above your head. Imagine a stream of blue light coming from the tip. Turn around clockwise in a complete circle, with your wand outstretched, all the time imagining the creation of a blue dome of light enclosing the room. As you do so, say:

I draw a circle of power, that it may be a meeting place of love and joy and truth, a boundary between the realms of men and the realms of the mighty ones, a circle to keep out all evil, and a circle to contain the power that we may raise within it.

This is called 'drawing the circle'. This circle can also be mentally drawn around yourself at any time when you feel you need protection, such as if you are being 'got at' by verbal or mental attack or even when you need to keep an unpleasant work colleague at bay.

CALLING ON THE ELEMENTS

To complete the casting of your circle, you must call upon the Guardian Spirits that represent the Elements. There are various ways of doing this, including drawing an appropriate pentagram at each quarter with your athame, while saying: 'I call upon the Guardian Spirits of [name the Element] to witness my rites and to guard my circle.'

The way I was taught was handed down indirectly from a hereditary witch and I am happy to share it. Going to the Eastern quarter first, take the incense, which is the offering to the Spirits of Air, hold it up by the eastern candle and say: 'Wind to the Way's call'. Offering the candle at the South say: 'Sun to the Way's call'. At the West it is 'Water' and at the North, 'Earth'. Travel clockwise to each point and, as you make your call, visualise either an appropriate wild place (such as a rushing stream for water) or what you think these Elemental spirits look like. As you do this, everyone with you should turn in the direction that you are addressing. Your circle is now cast. If anyone needs to go out of the circle, cut an imagined door in it with your athame or wand and close it again after the person has passed through.

At the end of the ritual, you must close your circle, either by thanking and saying goodbye to the Spirits or by holding up the original offering for a few seconds by way of thanks, visualising again, and then returning it to the altar.

CALLING ON THE GODDESS AND GOD

You are now ready to call upon or 'invoke' the Goddess and God to be with you in your circle. These words for the Goddess are based on those

from the old Book of Shadows: use them as they are or make up your own, according to the festival that you are celebrating.

I/We call upon you, Mighty Mother of us all,
Bringer of all fruitfulness,
By seed and root,
By bud and stem,
By leaf and flower and fruit.
I/We invite you to my/our circle here
That I/we may touch with your hands,
Speak with your tongue,
And kiss with your lips,
So that within me/us your service may be fulfilled.

And for the God:

Horned One, Lord of Life and Death,
Of day and night,
Of the sun and of the trees,
I/We invite you to our circle here
That I/we may learn the courage of your heart,
The joy of your passion,
And love of life from your fire of creation,
And so walk forever in your ways.

When calling upon the Goddess, it is traditional to stand with your feet slightly apart and your arms out to the sides at shoulder level, palms raised. For calling upon the God stand with feet together and your hands crossed on your chest, palms towards you.

CAKES AND WINE

The eating of cakes and wine towards the end of a ritual is not an imitation of a communion service of any other religion. It firstly celebrates the joyous relationship between male and female: the male and female deities, the relationship between male and female partners and also the interwoven male and female aspects that are in all of us. The athame and the chalice become representations of male and female when the wine is blessed; this act is also known as 'The Great Rite'. Celebrating with cakes and wine also has other purposes. Eating together binds a company together and makes a happy occasion. Thirdly, eating or drinking something brings you back to earthly reality after concentrating on the spiritual plane.

If you are working alone, leave the chalice on the altar. Hold your wand or athame with both hands with blade or tip pointing downwards. Gradually lower it into the chalice, saying: 'As the athame to the male, the chalice is to the female, and so conjoined they bring truth and blessedness.' Then lift the chalice, say, 'Blessed be' and take a sip. Working with a partner of the opposite sex, the man holds the chalice and the woman the athame. The words are the same. The woman drinks first and hands the chalice to the man saying, 'Blessed be' again. Working with a person of the same sex, simply choose who holds the chalice or athame. With a group, after the first two have drunk, the chalice is passed round clockwise, the person handing it on saying, 'Blessed be' to the next.

Next, the plate of food is held up and the words here are: 'May this food bring us health, wealth, joy and peace, and that fulfilment of love which brings everlasting happiness.' The person holding the food up takes a piece and passes the plate on clockwise, again saying, 'Blessed be'.

The contents of the chalice can be anything that you choose that makes a pleasant drink. I have suggested a different recipe for each of the festivals. However, if you don't drink alcohol, use an appropriate fruit juice (grape instead of wine, or apple instead of cider). Similarly

with the cakes, you can either make them yourself, or use something you have bought. I have often used Jaffa Cakes, or cereal bars cut into moon shapes. No one is a super-person and making things may sometimes be inconvenient. Do what you can and enjoy it, rather than worrying over the oven.

WINDING DOWN

If you are working in a group, after the cakes and wine, offer people the opportunity of contributing something themselves, such as singing an appropriate song, playing an instrument, telling a story or reading a poem. It is a good way of sharing talents, but don't make it compulsory. Not everyone is a performer. This can also be a time for quiet conversation and the sharing of successes or problems. When things come to a natural end, close the circle.

AND THEN...

Enjoy yourselves, have a party, share a feast to which everybody has contributed, play more music, sing more songs, whatever the occasion calls for.

IF THINGS GO WRONG

If someone muddles their words, blows the candle out by mistake or drops something, don't be afraid to laugh. The God and Goddess will probably laugh with you. Festivals are joyous occasions and small mishaps and laughter will never take away the true meaning of your intentions.

CHAPTER 1

SAMHAIN

Samhain (pronounced 'sow-ane') begins at sunset on 31 October and lasts through to midnight on 1 November. Your circle and celebrations can be on either day.

The name 'Samhain' is Irish Gaelic for the month of November (see Janet and Stewart Farrar's *Eight Sabbats for Witches*). Hallowe'en, as the day is more commonly known in Britain and America, comes from the name of the Christian festival of All Hallows (also called All Saints or All Souls), which was held on November 1 to counteract the Pagan associations of that time of the year. October 31 was All Hallows Eve, which soon became shortened to Hallowe'en. Other names are the Festival of Remembrance, the Feast of Apples, Ancestor Night or the Feast of the Dead.

THE FESTIVAL AND ITS MEANING

Samhain marks the beginning of winter. It is a festival of contrasts, an ending and a beginning. It is a time of great solemnity and remembrance but also of fun and laughter, games and feasting, cutting pumpkins and lighting bonfires. We look back over the past year and look forward to the future, leaving our past behind and resting from inner tasks and quests. We face the darkness, but look forward to the new light that is not far behind. Both death and life are celebrated in their many forms. We remember and honour those who have died and welcome their spirits and the spirits of those who are waiting to be reborn. You may be celebrating alone or with a few friends, but many other people are celebrating too, in their own way, from the children out 'trick or treating' to the elderly preparing for winter and looking back over their memories. It is a time for the Old Religion and for new customs. You could say that all of life (and death) is here in this one night, a night that sets itself apart from all other days in the year. It's a strange night, a weird and wild night, but one of the best in the year.

Samhain is a festival through which many aspects of Paganism and Wicca can be explained and, as befits a night of contrasts, some of the lessons are easy and others more difficult to explain!

Samhain, in the old Celtic farming calendar, marked the end of the summer season and the beginning of winter. The cattle had been brought into barns, the grain was all in store, whether the harvest had been good or meagre, and the last crops put away were the apples and berries. All outside work on the land was finished. The past year was therefore completed. Beginning was the time of threshing and milling and of planning and preparation for the coming year.

The evidence of the coming winter is everywhere at Samhain. In fields, woods and parks, the leaves are brown and falling fast, birds are migrating, and the first frosts are here or not far away. It seems like the end of all birth and life, but small, tight buds are on the twigs, seeds are sleeping in brown earth and foxes are seeking their mates. As one cycle ends, another is ready to begin.

In our own personal year, we have seen through the tasks and projects that we set ourselves when the light was beginning to grow. Now, we put our old year behind us and begin the new in a time of quiet contemplation and meditation, which will prepare us for new ventures when the time is right. As the God rests and sleeps in the Land of Shadows, so we mentally rest and sleep. This doesn't mean that we all refuse to work and go into hibernation (nice as this idea may seem when we set out for work on a cold, dark November morning!), but, in

terms of our inner quest and spiritual journey, we use this time to recharge our batteries. No new tasks are identified or set at this time but we leave our minds open to absorb new inspirations and thoughts. On Samhain night, we bid farewell to the old year and wish each other luck and happiness in the new.

If it is your intention to work through the celebrations in the order that they are placed in this book, and you have not done anything like this before, beginning with an ending may seem strange, and some of the rituals and meditations may seem irrelevant or unfamiliar to you at this moment. But you can't have a beginning without an ending and this one night marks them both. Read the rituals and take in their meaning. Carry out any that seem right for you now and then open your mind to thoughts and ideas during the dark days of rest and look forward to growing and changing when the new light comes. This is the beginning of your new understanding.

GODDESS AND GOD

At Samhain, the Goddess is in her Crone aspect, the old wise woman who will bring her gifts of insight and divination. She sits by her cauldron, taking our old lives and transforming them ready for rebirth. With the cutting of the corn and the dying of the leaves, the God has descended from our world into the Underworld, Otherworld or Shadowlands, where he becomes the Lord of the Shadows, and where he rests before rebirth. The Goddess meets him there as his Queen and their love for each other continues.

The God also takes the form of the leader of the Wild Hunt, riding through the skies with his pack of white, red-eared hounds, chasing the souls of the dead who are reluctant to leave this earth and taking them back with him to the Shadowlands.

THE BOUNDARY BETWEEN THE WORLDS

'The boundary between the worlds is thin.' That phrase has been said so often about Samhain, but what does it really mean? Most Wiccans accept that the world that we live in and experience every day is only one type of reality. There are others that are just as real that exist alongside our normal experience, but we are rarely aware of them. The Otherworld or Land of Shadows is on a separate plane from our real world, but there are certain times, such as turning points in the year, when the boundary becomes easier to cross. Samhain, when thoughts of death are very close and the Wheel is turning from an end to a beginning, is one of these times. Samhain is not to be feared, and spirits of those past and those yet to be born are welcomed into the circle. We must never ever call them back, however, for we do not know what is happening to them in their own world. Wrenching them away when they are going through something important could be harmful to them, so we must neither expect nor force, but simply leave a welcoming way open.

DEATH AND LIFE

Most Wiccans believe in reincarnation and that death is only a preparation for rebirth. After death in this world, a person's spirit will go to the Otherworld, Shadowlands or Summerlands (there are many names for it), first to rest and sleep and recover from the experiences they have had in this world, and then to reflect on the lessons that have been learned throughout their recent life. They may then choose to be reborn to progress a little more and learn more lessons (or even the same ones again). Some say that they can choose to whom they will be born and where. Certainly the wish of the old Celtic people and probably of those who lived even earlier, was to be reborn within the same tribe and even within the same family. Even now, at a Wiccan handfasting (marriage ceremony) the couple can choose to be soulmates, meaning that they will be together in the next life as well as

this. The length of time between death and rebirth varies considerably. It can be hundreds of years or just a few.

Death is a mystery that nobody can explain for certain, but our beliefs are reinforced by the stories of those who have had near-death experiences, fleeting memories of past lives and, more recently, past life regressions. We have probably all been in a 'déjà vu' situation at some time in our lives, and some people that we meet in this world for the first time seem so familiar that we feel we must have met them before. Reincarnation is an ancient belief that has been handed down in our collective unconscious for thousands of generations.

At Samhain, we remember past relations and friends, particularly those who have died during the past year. We welcome their presence and show them the way by placing a lighted candle in the window. This candle is said to guide good spirits and keep away bad ones, hence the lighted pumpkins whose crazy faces are designed to frighten away the unwelcome.

Another custom which also probably goes back to Celtic times is to lay a spare place at the table for any returning spirit, and putting out food or drink for them. This was described by Rosemary Sutcliffe in *The Eagle of the Ninth*. Some people place this plate outside the door. The food rarely disappears and becomes an offering to wildlife, but some say the essence has been taken and the welcome acknowledged. From these customs come the names Feast of the Dead and Ancestor Night.

Armistice Day, another Festival of Remembrance, is on November 11, twelve days afterwards. If it had not been for the calendar changes of 1752, when twelve days were removed to bring Britain into line with the rest of Europe, we may all have been laying our wreaths and lighting our candles on the same day. The spirit of both is the same.

The wild winds and dull days of the season complement our remembrances, but should not be depressing. We can sit by the fire and meditate and plan. The light and warmth will soon be reborn again and

so too will the spirits, if they so wish. Many of those who have died have now become those waiting to be reborn.

The night of Samhain is also the end of a year in our lives. In our own way, we are ready to begin anew. We offer ourselves to the Goddess in her guise as the Welsh deity Ceridwen who, with her cauldron of inspiration, will give us rebirth and a new start.

DIVINATION

Because it marks a new beginning, Samhain has always been a time for divination. Through all the years of the Christian church, the old customs were still performed at what had become Hallowe'en. Young girls, especially, tried to find out whom they would marry by various means. Lining up a row of hazelnuts along the front of the fire was a favourite. Each one was given the name of a possible suitor and the first nut to crack and jump indicated the future husband. Using just one nut was a way to find out a suitor's intentions, with the words:

If you love me, jump and fly,
If you hate me, lie and die.

Another way was to remove the peel of an apple in one long strip and throw it over your shoulder. If it formed the shape of a letter, it was the initial of your future partner. There were many other methods and some of the 'good luck' divinations became party games such as apple bobbing.

SAMHAIN AND FOLK CUSTOMS

Samhain is associated with fire, mischievous spirits and begging for treats, all of which are inter-related.

When an agricultural or gardening year comes to an end, there is always rubbish to burn. Hop bines, potato stalks and unwanted branches from coppiced or pruned trees were all burned on a seasonal bonfire, which both practically and ritually removed the remains of the old year. Burning fires also keep away the evil or mischievous spirits that are said to roam around at Samhain. Sometimes these fires are used for divination. The custom of Samhain bonfires was most prevalent early on in Wales, Scotland and the Isle of Man, but it became fairly universal throughout Britain after the discovery of the Gunpowder Plot and the various religious burnings which took place in the sixteenth and seventeenth centuries. In *The Return of the Native*, Thomas Hardy describes a November bonfire which was built on a barrow, or burial mound:

> The flames from funeral piles long ago kindled there had shone down upon the lowlands as these were shining now. Festival fires to Thor and Woden had followed on the same ground and duly had their day. Indeed, it is pretty well known that such blazes as this the heathmen were now enjoying are rather the lineal descendants from jumbled Druidical rites and Saxon ceremonies than the invention of popular feeling about Gunpowder Plot.

He goes on to say that lighting fires at this time of the year 'indicates a spontaneous, Promethean rebelliousness against the fiat that this recurrent season shall bring foul times, cold darkness, misery and death.' That just about says it all, really.

In Britain, there are various fire celebrations during October and November such as the bonfire processions in Sussex and Tar Barrel Rolling in Ottery St Mary, Devon. All have different origins, but all produce warmth, spectacle and enjoyment that fly in the face of winter. Go out and find them, or a local equivalent.

Punky Night

It's Punky Night, tonight,
It's Punky Night tonight,
Give us a candle, give us a light,
It's Punky Night tonight.

The rhyme, to the tune of 'The Farmer's in his Den' is chanted by children on the last Thursday in October, as they process round the village of Hinton St George in Somerset, carrying lighted turnip lanterns. The local legend is that it came from a time when all the men of the village went to a fair in a neighbouring town and got so drunk they couldn't find their way home. The women then had to go out looking for them with lanterns which, locally, were called 'punkies'. Maybe it is true, or maybe the custom goes way further back.

The name 'punky' could possibly come from the mischievous spirits that were once thought to trample or destroy any crops that remained unharvested at Samhain. They are also called the 'Pooka' or 'Phooka' and the lights from the lanterns kept them at bay.

Pumpkins

Pumpkins are another form of mischief-repelling vegetable lantern, much larger and more spectacular than turnips or swedes and definitely not so portable! They are easy to grow, but have a habit of taking over the vegetable patch with their long, twining stems, so be careful where you plant them! Pumpkins were originally grown in France and England in the sixteenth century, taken to America by the Pilgrim Fathers and have recently become totally associated with modern American Hallowe'en customs. It was probably the Americans who first thought of making them into lanterns, but now they are piled high in British supermarkets during the last two weeks of October. Pumpkin lanterns have become a new tradition for many families, whatever their religious persuasion, and Pagan homes are no exception.

TRICK OR TREAT

'Trick or treat' has also come over from America in recent years, but its origins are British. Many ancient celebrations or saints' days became an excuse for poor children to go round begging for food or money. Sometimes they sang a song or produced something like a garland of flowers in return and sometimes the request was accompanied by a threat. No treats for the ploughboys as they went round at the beginning of January meant that they ploughed up your front garden. At Samhain, or All Souls Night, children went round souling, or asking for small cakes called 'Soul Cakes'. In Scotland, and probably other places as well, there were rowdy threats from the older ones such as this verse, quoted by Ronald Hutton in *Stations of the Sun*:

> If ye dinna let us in
> We will bash yer windies (windows) in.

In time, these begging customs were forgotten in Britain, but they had been taken across the Atlantic where they survived into modern times, being refined and changed along the way. Now we have taken them up again. Small people running around dressed as ghoulies and ghosties are still imitating the 'pookas', so keep a bowl of sweets handy and join in the fun. If you think your circle is in danger of being interrupted by this, hold it on 1 November instead.

THINGS TO DO

THE SABBAT WHEEL

To help you remember the happenings and achievements of the past year, at some time between Mabon and Samhain use natural materials to make an eight-spoked wheel, bearing symbols of the different Sabbats. Thin willow branches or wheat straw are ideal materials. You

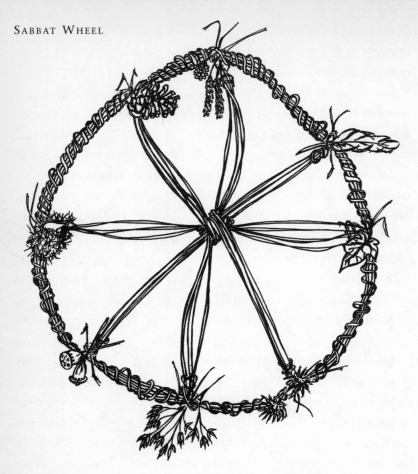

can also use 'withies' or raffia bought from a craft shop. I use rushes, which grow abundantly very close to my home. The species is the soft rush, *Juncus effusus*, which has long, smooth stems, no leaves and a head of small brown flowers growing out of the side of the stem. It is the type of rush that is often used for piling on carts for rushbearing celebrations that take place in the north of England at places such as Gorton, near Manchester, and at Sowerby Bridge. They were also once used for making rush lights and for strewing over floors.

To make the Sabbat Wheel, you will need only 28 long stems. Cut them rather than breaking them so that you do not tear the plant out

of the ground and, if possible, take them from several different clumps of rushes. Twelve stems will be used for the outer wheel and 16 for the crosspieces.

You will also need a small, natural symbol of each of the year's festivals. If you have no idea about this, go for a walk in the country with the clear idea in your head that you are out to find these symbols. It is surprising what you will find. The first time that I made this wheel, I didn't even have a clue as to what to make the base from. I left an irksome job at the computer and went out for a walk instead. Before long I came across the rushes and realised that they were exactly what I needed. In the old Celtic tree calendar, in which each lunar month is dedicated to a specific tree or plant, Samhain falls in the 'Reed Month', and I had been thinking about this as I set out. Having cut the rushes I thought about Ostara and Imbolc, which could have been tricky to represent in the autumn. I found a feather on the ground and some dried up alder catkins. A pine cone did for Yule and, back home, I cut a sprig of oats from my Mary Barleycorn for Lammas (see page 180). When I went up the garden to fill the bird-bath, a chestnut husk had dropped into it, so that did for Samhain. For Midsummer I used a dried flower and found some poppy seed heads for Mabon. An ivy leaf from the hedge served for Beltane. This all happened in the space of an hour. Someone was watching over me and helped me on my way, so I gave thanks for it. I do realise, though, that not everybody can simply walk out of the door into the countryside. You can also make your wheel from craft materials and make the symbols from paper or card. Another alternative is to draw a picture of the wheel with any objects or symbols which represent your year. Whatever you use and however you go about it, the inspiration will come from the same source.

If you are able to find rushes, take one and bend it round into a circle about 20cm in diameter. To fasten the ends, wind one end around the other for the whole of the overlap. Take another rush, secure the end by pushing it into the overlap of the first circle and keep winding it round the first rush until it is all used up. Continue doing this with another ten rushes until you have a thick circle, tucking in the ends as you go. You may find the circle becomes twisted but this will be remedied by the crosspieces.

For the first crosspiece, take four rushes. Place the ends together and join the rushes by making a knot through all the stems about 10cm from the end. With the first knot on the inside of the circle and the rest of the rushes placed across the diameter of the circle, tie the ends to the circle edge. Make another knot in the long remaining parts of the rushes where they meet the other side of the circle. Trim the ends to 10cm and tie them onto the side of the circle. You now have a crosspiece going across the diameter of the circle and secured at each side, with ends of about 5cm remaining attached to the knots. With another four rushes, attach another crosspiece to one side of the circle at right angles across the first. Before attaching it to the opposite side, wind it once around the centre of the first crosspiece. Attach two more crosspieces in the same way, making an eight-spoked wheel. Tie on your objects using the left over ends of rushes, putting them in the right order: Samhain, Yule, Imbolc, Ostara, Beltane, Litha, Lammas and Mabon. You will now see that the wheel has no beginning and no end.

Once the wheel is complete, hang it up in your home to dry. At Samhain or just after, ritually burn it or pull it apart to say goodbye to the old year.

MEDITATION ON THE WHEEL

Use the Sabbat Wheel or simply hold images of the different Sabbats in your mind, then take some time to sit and reflect on the events in your life over the past twelve months. Think of how you were and what you experienced at the time of each festival. Be pleased at and give thanks for your achievements and view the disappointments and sorrows not as failures but as lessons learned or experience gained, which will help you in the future. You may have changed considerably over the year,

both inwardly and outwardly, or you may simply have experienced a small change in attitude known only to yourself. There are also many stages in between and all are part of the progression and the journey through life. Whatever has happened in the past year and whatever the consequences, it is time to make a new start by building on your achievements and the lessons learned.

Draw and cast your circle. Call upon the Goddess and God in the following way:

I call upon you, Great Goddess,

As the Wise Crone,

The keeper of the Cauldron of Death and Rebirth,

And the Turner of the Wheel.

Cailleach, Ceridwen, Baba Yaga, Hecate,

I ask your presence at this turning of the year.

Show me the lessons I have learned and need to learn,

Remind me of the joys and sorrows that each season has brought.

Take into your cauldron the self that I was in the past year,

And turn it into the new self that I will become.

I call upon you, Dark Lord of the Shadows,

Old Wise Man and Leader of the Hunt,

Herne, Cernunnos, Osiris, Hades,

I ask your presence at this turning of the year.

Gather up the parts of my life that need to be shed,

Take them to the Land of Shadows

That my new self may be reborn with the light.

Hold up the Sabbat Wheel or picture that you have made. Say the following, stopping after each description of a Sabbat and thinking about that particular time in your life. Give thanks, note the lessons or whatever you need to do, then let it go. Don't make any judgements.

Don't make any promises or resolutions to yourself. These will come later after you have had time to rest in the dark of winter.

The Wheel brings memories of the year that is done,
Of the turning seasons and the path of the Sun.

At Yule we watched the life's new spark
Glowing and growing in winter's dark.

At Imbolc, Brighid was welcomed in,
Goddess of the arts and messenger of spring.

Ostara's Hare brought eggs and the Sun,
It was time to grow, the light had won.

At Beltane we danced round Jack-in-the-Green,
And crowned with flowers was the Goddess Queen.

The Sun at Litha was at its height,
But the Holly King did win the fight.

Lammas brought harvest and the first baked bread,
But the Goddess mourned, the God was dead.

Mabon celebrated harvest home,
The corn all stored, the year's work done.

At Samhain we welcome the unseen guest.
The wheel has turned, it's time to rest.

These are the memories of the Sabbat Wheel.
May they bring joy, and the sadness heal.

We send out thanks for success and pleasure,

And take the lessons as jewels to treasure.

If you have an open fire, you can burn the Wheel on it now. If you have made a bonfire outside, put the Wheel on that at the end of the evening. If burning is impossible, take the Wheel to an outdoor location, gently pull it apart and cast the pieces to the four winds. As you burn or take apart the Wheel, say:

What is past is past, we look to the new.

Wheel of the past year, burn for us now [or, be scattered now].

FOOD FOR THE WINTER

The summer's harvest provides food for the long winter days. You have reaped your harvest of achievements and lessons and stored them safely in your heart. Now is the time to begin using them to enrich your life.

In your Book of Shadows, write down the things that you think you have achieved and learned over the past year and beside them write down how they will affect your life for the better. Now sit and imagine yourself in everyday situations where they might be of use and promise yourself to call on them.

You will also find yourself using them unexpectedly and this is always a source of pleasure and surprise, particularly when all it has taken is a shift of attitude to make you react differently (and more favourably) to the world. Try to make a note of them when you can.

THE SAMHAIN FIRE

Lighting a fire at Samhain is a symbolic way of maintaining warmth and cheer all through the dark days. It's great to have a bonfire outside but, as well as or instead of (if you don't have the space), light a candle in a cauldron indoors. What we usually do is light both, the candle as a part of the ritual and then the bonfire afterwards. As it is near to November

5, we also set off a few fireworks to round off the evening. If you build the bonfire in advance, check for hedgehogs before you light it!

For the indoor part, you will need a large candle in a cauldron, fixed either with Blu-tack, or in a small holder. Light the candle early in the evening, so that it remains a focus point. If this is part of a complete ritual, put the cauldron in the centre of the circle. As the candle is lit, one person says:

We light the Samhain fire.

It will light us through the dark days, warm us in the cold,

Take the place of Sun's rays, shining out like gold.

It will cheer us when the mood is low, thaw the hardened heart

Melting ice and frost and snow, laughing at the dark.

Into yourself now take the flame, hold it in your mind.

All through the days of the sun's wane it will be there to find.

Sit and watch the flame for a few minutes so that you will be able to remember it when you feel that winter is getting on top of you.

REMEMBRANCE AND WELCOME

Remembering loved ones who have died and welcoming their presence can be done when you are alone or in a group. Start by remembering any people close to you who have died this past year. These are the ones who are most likely to hear your call. You can include loved pets if you wish. Then you can work 'outwards' to loved ones who have died longer than a year ago but who are still very much in your thoughts. Candles can also be lit for any significant person, not related or close to you, who has died during the year and whom you admired, or for people killed as a result of tragedy. In these cases, you are not calling back but remembering with reverence. When working in a group, try not to get too outrageous. When it gets to what I call the 'long dead hamster stage' I call a halt. However, always try to respect other people's feelings and what they are trying to do.

You will need a large, sturdy cooking pot filled with earth or sand and a number of small candles. Birthday cake candles are ideal if there are a lot of people. If you are alone or with one or two others, you can use 10cm candles. The first person to light a candle will put it into the centre of the pot. Others will gradually work outwards to the edges. This does not mean that the first person's candle is the most important; it is simply the safest way of doing it (reaching over other lighted candles gives you a burnt wrist). You will also need a plate of food, such as a small amount of bread and cheese.

Work within a cast circle. Place the Samhain candle and the pot of earth in the centre of the circle, together with a pile of small candles. One person says:

Tonight the veil between the worlds is thin.

We remember loved ones gone from this world.

We offer them a place in our hearts

And in our circle of love.

If they choose to come, they are welcome.

[Hold up the plate of food.]

We offer them food.

We guide them by flickering flame.

In turn, each person takes a candle, lights it from the Samhain fire and places it in the earth, saying:

I light this candle in memory of [naming the person and, if they choose, describing them and saying why they were so special to them].

When all the candles are burning together, say, sing or chant the following rhyme (a tune that works is that of the skipping rhyme, 'The High Skip').

Banish dark with the light,
See the candles burning bright.
Candles burn, candles flame,
To recall your loved one's name.
See the candles burning there,
Send your love into the air,
Send it out into the night,
Glowing with the candle's light.

At this point, we remember all those who were persecuted and who died during the witch trials. If anyone knows the song, 'The Burning Times', it is very appropriate to sing it here. One person says:

With thoughts of love

We remember the nine million,

Children of the Goddess and God, who died for the Way.

We honour their courage,

Their passion, their commitment,

And offer them a place by our fire.

The following words are from the original Book of Shadows, slightly altered. Read them here if you like:

Dread Lord of the Shadows,

God of Life and the Giver of Life,

Open wide the gates through which all must pass.

Let our dear ones, who have gone before,

Return this night to make merry with us.

And when our time comes, as it must,

We will enter your realms gladly and unafraid,

For we know that, rested and refreshed among our dear ones,

We will be reborn again by your grace

And by the grace of the Great Mother.

Let it be in the same time and same place as our beloved ones,

That we may meet, and know and remember, and love them again.

Now comes the joyful bit, when all Spirits are welcomed. This small but effective chant was handed down to me. On the last line, everybody shouts out loud and the atmosphere of solemnity gives way to enjoyment.

All Hallows Light

Ring about, Ring about,

Where the Way was and is,

Are there more of ye about?

Leave the candles burning until they go out. Put the food by the altar then place it outside when you go to bed.

BURNING THE YEAR'S DEBRIS

If over the past year, we have noticed something about ourselves that we do not like, then we can symbolically burn it on the Samhain fire. Work within a cast circle. You will need a pencil and small square of plain paper for each person, and a large, flameproof container of water, such as a saucepan or heavy casserole. Place the Samhain candle and the water in the centre of the circle. One person says:

Look at the fire.

What parts of your life are you ready to burn?

Your fears, your angers, your negative thoughts?

The God goes to his death to be reborn again,

The Crone Goddess will return as a young girl.

Although we constantly journey into the sacred spiral,

Never to return on the same path again,

Parts of our lives can be renewed.

We can send into the dark the parts of us that we do not like,

So that, in the spring,

We will see unexpected parts of our lives emerging and being born
To give us joy and hope.

Everyone writes on their piece of paper the aspect of themselves that they would like to change or get rid of. In turn, light them from the Samhain candle and, when the paper has safely burned far enough, drop them into the water. If you are lighting a fire in the garden, you may like to keep the pieces of paper to throw on that later. When all the pieces have been burned, everyone says:

These old parts of ourselves we banish now
What's past is past, we look to the new.

APPLES

If you cut an apple in half crossways, you will see that the seeds are arranged in a five-pointed star, which, like the pentagram, represents Earth, Air, Fire, Water and Spirit. Apples have long been used for divining purposes, and we can use them to discover how many new tasks or projects we should set ourselves as a part of our inner journey in the coming year. Cut an apple in half and count the seeds. Each seed represents one choice or pathway. If you only have one, it may mean that you should concentrate all your efforts on one important thing. If you have several, then you can and should work on several tasks at once. If you can't find any, maybe you need to go over again some of the projects that you set yourself for this year, or maybe you are just starting on the path. In which case, ideas will come to you in the next few months. Use the number as a guide to meditation, not as something set in stone.

You will need apples for everyone and your athame, or other knife to cut them with. One person holds up an apple and says:

Deep inside the fruit

Are the seeds of new life.

New dreams, new plans, new attitudes, new thoughts.

Hold them within you through the year's darkest days,

Then plant them and love them.

With the light they will grow.

Everyone present takes an apple, cuts it, counts the seeds and then eats every part of it, including the seeds.

After your ritual, write in your Book of Shadows how many seeds you found and think about what they might mean.

I wrote the following song for a Hallowe'en entertainment at a country park that was devised as a walk in the woods. The audience came across the Apple Woman at her table who invited them to see their future in an apple. The tune is 'Do You Love an Apple?'.

Take a ripe apple and cut it in two,

There'll be a star in the middle for you.

Chorus (after every verse)

Find the star, the five-pointed star,

It holds a secret whoever you are.

If you're looking for pathways, you need not look far,

Just count the seeds in the points of the star.

If one, two, three, four or five seeds do appear,

That's how many new pathways you'll travel next year.

Think of the things you would most like to do,

Then eat all the apple, your wish will come true.

Altar and decorations

Some people like black for Samhain, but others prefer orange, which seems to have become a significant colour, probably because it is the colour of pumpkins. A black cloth with orange candles is great, or you

can do it the other way round or use just one colour. If you have enough small pumpkins, cut moon and star shapes from them, rather than scary faces, and use them to mark the quarters. Decorate the house with autumn leaves, dried bracken and bowls of apples and chestnuts.

SAMHAIN INCENSE

2 teaspoons myrrh

1 teaspoon juniper berries, crushed

1 teaspoon allspice berries, crushed

½ teaspoon sandalwood powder, if available (sanderswood raspings if not)

1 bay leaf, crumbled

4 drops patchouli oil

2 drops sandalwood oil

CAKES AND WINE

Mulled cider

Because of the association of apples with Samhain, make mulled cider and keep it in a flask until you are ready to use it.

1 pint/575ml medium cider

2 tablespoons honey

2 cinnamon sticks

2 teaspoons allspice berries

Put all the ingredients into a saucepan and stir on a low heat for the honey to dissolve. Bring them to just below simmering point and hold them there for 10 minutes.

Dark Moon cakes

3oz/100g ground almonds

3oz/100g wholemeal flour

1 egg

2 tablespoons clear honey

Black food colouring

Heat the oven to 350°F/180°C/gas 4. Mix the almonds and flour in a bowl. Make a well in the centre and put in the egg, honey and about 1 teaspoon food colouring. Using a wooden spoon, mix everything together. Add a little more food colouring if necessary. The mixture will be quite stiff. Form it into about 30 crescent Moon shapes. Put them onto a baking sheet and bake them for ten minutes or until they are firm. Immediately lift them onto a plate, using a spatula.

THE COMPLETE SAMHAIN RITUAL

Cast the circle. Invoke the Goddess and God (page 18). One person says:

> The leaves fall from the trees
>
> And the world prepares for sleep.
>
> Darkness gathers,
>
> Nothing grows,
>
> All is still.
>
> It is the end of the old year.
>
> The Sun God goes to the Shadows,
>
> The Goddess weeps amber tears.
>
> But the Wheel of the Year is a circle
>
> And circles have no end.
>
> The God goes only to the Summerlands
>
> To rest and sleep before rebirth.
>
> We too descend into the darkness to be reborn with the light
>
> This is not an end, but a beginning.

Then use the ideas suggested earlier in this chapter to cover all the following activities:

- Light the Samhain candle
- The Samhain Wheel (include the calls to the Goddess and God)
- Burning the year's debris
- Remembrance and welcome
- Apples
- Cakes and wine – when the chalice has gone round the circle, the first person holds it up and says: 'To the Old Ones. Merry meet and merry part, and merry meet again.' If anyone would like to sing an appropriate song or tell a story, put these in here.

Blessing
Samhain is:

A time of endings,

A time of the thinning of the veil,

A time to honour and welcome the Old Ones,

A time to clear out fears,

A time for inner peace and rest.

It is:

Pumpkins and apples,

Hazelnuts and cider,

Love, and remembering, and friendship.

May the Goddess as Wise Woman and the God as Lord of the Shadows make us blessed this Samhain night, and guide us through the dark days until we come once again to the light.

Close the circle
If you have a bonfire and fireworks outside, go out and enjoy them, and burn your Samhain wheel and your pieces of paper. Play the apple bobbing game indoors. Indoor fireworks are also a good idea.

CHAPTER 2

YULE

Yule can be at any time from 20 to 23 December, depending on the precise movements of the Sun. Consult an astrological diary for the precise date.

'Yule' has both Norse and Saxon origins. *Lul* is Norse for 'wheel', and *Hweolor-tid* is Saxon for 'turning time'.

THE FESTIVAL AND ITS MEANING

Yule is one of the most joyful of festivals because, in the middle of the dark and cold, it gives us a glimpse of longer days and the promise of spring and new beginnings.

In the Wiccan calendar, Yule marks the turn of the Wheel from the waning to the waxing year. We celebrate the return of the Sun, the rebirth of the God, the renewal of the Goddess and the victory of the Oak King over the Holly King. We contemplate our hopes and aspirations for the coming year and consider how our natural gifts and talents can be used for good. We also hang out lights, decorate a tree, bring in evergreens, burn a Yule log, give presents, sing, dance, perform a piece of ritual drama and have a party.

Yule is the festival most rich in remembered tradition and ritual. In the early days of Christianity people were reluctant to give up their Pagan path and the Midwinter celebrations. It was therefore decided that the birth of Christ should be celebrated at the same time. This

enabled the ritual dramas, songs and decorations to be continued with added Christian meanings. You do not have to look far beneath the surface to discover the old Pagan links and we have a wonderful pool of songs, words and traditions with which to enrich the festival.

The dark days leading up to Yule should be a time of quiet contemplation. We think not only of what has happened to us over the past year, but of the projects that we would like to see happen and the personal goals that we might want to achieve in the coming months. At Samhain, we cleared away the old year and received the gift of seeds for the new. We have kept those seeds dormant within us over the past six weeks. Now it is time to think about what they are and how we are going to make them grow. There are two meditations in this chapter, which relate to this 'seed planting' time. The second, 'Labelling the seeds and sowing the seeds', is a bit like making New Year resolutions, but is much kinder to yourself and easier to follow through.

What is now known as the 'Christmas period' is a kind of 'time out' for many people. The normal routine is set aside for a few days whilst we celebrate, see friends and rest. This is an ideal opportunity to take time to think about new projects and aspirations without suddenly going overnight from dark meditations to actions of regrowth. Everything seems to stand still for a while, before you get into gear and pull away, so take advantage of it. By Twelfth Night, January 6, you will be ready to grow with the waxing year with strength and courage.

GODDESS AND GOD

At Yule, the Goddess can be experienced in all her three aspects. In the darkest days she is still the wise old crone, meditating on the past year, sleeping and waiting, and dreaming of a new world to come. Yule is the time for her renewal and she magically becomes both the young

Mother of the God and also a child herself, a twin to the God, who will grow with him in the spring and become his lover at Beltane.

Since Samhain, the God has been in the Summerlands, resting, sleeping and preparing for rebirth. At Yule, he is reborn of the Goddess so he can grow in strength with the Sun.

A FESTIVAL OF DARK AND LIGHT

Yule is a festival of contrasts. The days before are noticeably very dark and often very still. It is as if the Earth is holding its breath and waiting for something to happen. Then, in the middle of winter, in the very darkest day of the year, we celebrate the returning light. By 6 January, mornings and evenings are becoming noticeably lighter.

Yule is therefore a festival of contrasts and its rituals often begin with quiet contemplation in semi-darkness and end with bright candles, gifts and celebrations.

WELCOME THE SUN

The festival of Yule marks the Winter Solstice, when, after the shortest day and the longest night, the Sun begins its return to the Earth.

Without the Sun, crops cannot grow and life on Earth would be impossible. Twelve thousand years ago, which is probably about when the earliest celebrations took place, the ever-darkening days must have seemed intolerable. Rituals were performed to entice the Sun back to the Earth. Then, as if by magic, the light began to grow again bringing a promise of warmer months. It must truly have been a time for rejoicing and renewed hope. Very early on, people gained an intimate knowledge of the stars and planets, and stone circles and wooden henges were constructed which directed the first of the Sun's rays on Solstice morning towards significant altars and stone carvings. The male Sun had returned to fertilise the Mother Earth.

Even though we may now feast on imported food bought from supermarkets, it still can't be produced without the warmth of the Sun.

We could not live without its light. Welcoming back the Sun is just as appropriate now as it ever was. The only difference is that now we know that the Sun will come back whether we celebrate or not.

THE HOLLY KING AND THE OAK KING

Besides the rebirth of the God from the Goddess, there is another 'God story' attached to Yule – the fight between the Oak King and the Holly King. The Oak King rules the waxing year and the Holly King rules the waning year. At the two Solstices, those of Midsummer and Midwinter, the two kings fight for supremacy. The Holly King wins at Midsummer and the Oak King at Yule.

We can only conjecture how this story was played out in the original Pagan rituals. Did two people fight for real? Was there a sacrifice, or was it only symbolic? Nobody knows. What is generally thought to be true is that the old story of the death and resurrection of the two rulers of the year was passed down through the Mummers plays, which are still traditionally performed during the Christmas period. What was once a significant seasonal ritual became entertainment for the rich and an opportunity to make a little extra cash for the poor, who would perform the play in front of the lord of the manor in Medieval times and, in later centuries, in the local pub and at the 'big houses'. The characters changed over the years. The Crusades produced St George and the Turkish Knight. A series of Georges on the throne of England turned St George into King George. Various foreign adversaries produced assailants such as Bold Slasher and the Prince of Paradine. Political and topical characters came in and out over the years, but the theme remained the same. Once the stage has been set and cleared by a 'Molly' or 'Enter-In', the characters fight, one (usually the 'goodie') goes down but is revived by a Doctor. They fight again and the other goes down. The Doctor cannot or will not revive him so in comes an ordinary person who produces a magic bottle of potion and the dead man rises up again. Jokes, antics and jollification abound and often the

Devil and Father Christmas appear at the end to collect money.

On page 63 is a short, ritual drama in which I have gone one step back from the classic Mummers play to produce a story of the Oak King and Holly King, but keeping the rhyming couplets and some of the wording. The Oak King wins but, if you walk in the countryside at Yule, you will not see much evidence of this. It is the holly's branches, along with ivy, that decorate our homes until Twelfth Night. I have therefore made him into the Lord of Misrule and given him Ivy as a consort. The Lord of Misrule was a person who, in Medieval times, was elected to run the Christmas festivities of a manor, court or big house for the Twelve Days of Christmas. He had an enormous amount of licence to do as he pleased. Come Twelfth Night, the decorations will come down, buds on branches will begin to swell and holly and ivy will lose their importance.

The other characters in the play, the robin and the wren, are the symbolic birds of the two Kings. The time of the wren comes to an end at Yule and the reign of the robin begins. Until very recent years, the wren was hunted and killed on Boxing Day and brought home with song and ceremony to ensure good luck for the coming year. The hunt no longer happens, but the songs still survive and are sung by folk singers, Morris dancers and Mummers all over the country.

YULE AND FOLK CUSTOMS

YULE PRESENTS

The gifts that we give each other at Yule and Christmas are tokens of love and friendship. They should also encourage us to think of our natural gifts or talents that have been granted to us, so that we can appreciate them and learn how to use them for our own and other people's good. On the night of the Solstice, you can dress someone up as Father Yule, dressed in a green cloak instead of red but still carrying

his sack of gifts, one for each person present. On page 68 there is a speech for him that reminds us why we are receiving these gifts. Once again, it is based on the words of Mummers' plays.

LIGHTS AND CANDLES

Lights and candles are becoming increasingly popular as part of the essential Christmas decorations. This 'lighting up', either with electricity or flame, goes back to the time when bonfires were lit to encourage the Sun back to the earth. Join in the fun. Join in your town's 'switching on' celebrations, hang lights round your house, burn an advent candle or buy a large candle that you light for the first time on Solstice night and burn every day until January 6. On page 58 is a ritual to welcome the Sun back to the Earth, to honour the God and Goddess and bring light and warmth into your home.

EVERGREENS

Holly, ivy, yew, bay and rosemary are all evergreen trees. In the old days, their green leaves were symbols of hope for the new green shoots and leaves that appear in the spring. Since very early times they have been used as decorations to bring their message of hope indoors. Holly is the masculine plant of the Holly King, used for luck and as a guardian against evil spirits. Ivy is feminine and once used in divination. Bay, in Roman times, was sacred to the Sun God Apollo and for the Celts was a symbol of health and strength which also kept away evil spirits. Mistletoe has always been a sacred plant with magical and healing powers. Matters of law were settled under its branches and those who passed beneath it exchanged a kiss of peace. Evergreen wreaths for the door, being wheel-shaped, are symbols of the ever-turning year. Use evergreens to decorate your house and your altar.

THE YULE TREE

The pine tree is another symbol of continuing life through winter's

dark days. In ancient times, trees were hung with offerings to the tree spirit and also with symbols representing wishes for the coming year. To the Native Americans, the pine tree is a symbol of peace. Bringing a living tree into the house is like bringing in a part of the forest, with its special scent and its atmosphere of peace and joy. Some people object to sacrificing a tree for the sake of tradition but, if you treat it well and either plant it or recycle it afterwards, it will give far more pleasure than an artificial tree.

YULE AND CHRISTMAS

The commemoration of Christ's birthday also means that much of the world is celebrating at this time of the year and, tackiness and commercialism apart, the feeling created by millions of people wishing each other peace and goodwill is positive and uplifting. Yule can be your only celebration of the season, or it can be the first in a long succession of festive days that stretch into the New Year. Christmas is traditionally celebrated for 12 days, but Yule celebrations can last, if you wish, for 16, until the decorations are taken down at Twelfth Night!

THINGS TO DO

GO FOR THE ENJOYMENT

The time between Samhain and Yule, as the days get gradually darker, should be a time of rest, contemplation and anticipation, almost like hibernation. However, shopping, writing cards, catching the post, finishing those jobs for which Yule or Christmas always acts as a significant deadline, cooking, attending carol services and nativity plays, putting up decorations, making up extra beds for visitors all seem to conspire against this happening. It actually depends on how you look at it.

Most of these tasks are only performed at this time of the year. They are in themselves small rituals, which distract us from the usual everyday cares of the world. Why do we do them? We buy presents for family and friends to show them that we care or to thank them for kindnesses during the year. Cards are sent to make contact, to thank and to confirm love and friendship. We cook to celebrate the return of the Earth's fertility and to provide families and friends with something to mark a special day. We go to hear carols and watch school plays to support our children and to remind us of our own childhood. The decorations, as we have seen, all have their own significance.

As you perform each task, think of the good reasons for doing it. This alone should take away some of the stresses and make you feel more positive about what is, after all, a 'season of peace and goodwill'. A task will take the same time, whether it is enjoyed or resented, so go for the enjoyment!

TAKE A STILLNESS BREAK

One of the characteristics of the two or three days leading up to Yule is an atmosphere that is there for everybody to appreciate. All you need to do is to stop and be alone, even for a few minutes. Sense the stillness in the air. The Earth seems to be withdrawing completely in on itself as the inward spiral into the dark is almost completed. This happens whatever the weather and whatever events or bustle are going on in the world around us. So take a break. You can sit quietly in front of a candle, gaze through the window at the sky, or go for a solitary walk. It doesn't have to take long and it can be at any time of the day. Just feel what is happening and enjoy the stillness.

WAITING FOR THE LIGHT

Ideally, you need to be alone for this one and sure that you will not be interrupted. Take as long or short a time as you like. Sit

comfortably, close your eyes and relax. Take three deep breaths. Imagine that you were alive 12,000 years ago. It is winter. You are cold and probably hungry. The days are getting shorter. You light a fire, sit by it and think about the past year, its successes and failures. In an earthenware pot in the corner of your dwelling are the carefully preserved seeds that will become next year's harvest. These seeds would have meant life and death for you and your tribe. As you are now, they are the projects and ideas that you have held within you since Samhain. Think about them. Which ones do you really want to grow? As the days get darker you wait, and wonder if the Sun will ever return for you to plant your seeds. Then suddenly, when it seems that the world cannot get any darker, a beam of strong, pale sunlight streams into your living space and lights up the seeds. They glow with a promise of the coming spring. See that light for one minute, before the Sun moves higher in the sky to illuminate a new day.

LABELLING THE SEEDS AND SOWING THE SEEDS
During the week after Yule, take time to think about and identify the seeds that you have held within you since Samhain, the seeds that were illuminated by the Sun in 'Waiting for the light' above (although it is not necessary for you to have done this meditation). They are the seeds of projects or opportunities, of personal development, of career moves, of life changes, of small, subtle shifts of attitude, of improved relationships, of anything that you think would improve your life and wellbeing and those of others around you. These projects can be big or small and can relate to any aspect of your life that you wish to improve and grow. Always remember that your work in this way has to be for the good of all and with harm to none, so do not include manipulating other people in your seeds.

On 30 December, in your Book of Shadows, draw as many seed packets as you need or feel you can cope with at this time. If this is the

first time that you have done anything like this, stick with one or two. Label them and maybe even draw pictures on the packets. As you draw, say:

These are the seeds I hold within,
Seeds that will grow with the coming spring.
I give them love as they do sleep,
To prepare them for the earth so deep.

Look at the drawings, think about your seeds and repeat the lines every day for a week.

By Twelfth Night, January 6, the days are getting noticeably longer. This is a good day on which to plant your seeds. In your Book of Shadows, draw pictures of your seeds under the earth. Label them. Draw the Sun and its warm rays shining down on the seeds and say this rhyme.

I plant my seeds in earth so bare
And nurture them with love and care.
May they grow tall and strong with the light
Through Sun and rain, through day and night.
For the good of all my planting's done.
I make this wish with harm to none.

Look at your drawing every day for a week, and say the rhyme to yourself. Then do it once a week until Imbolc.

WELCOMING BACK THE SUN

This can be done as a solitary ritual, by simply lighting the single candle or as a communal celebration in which everyone lights their own candle. You will need a cauldron or metal pot of some description, a new orange candle, Blu-tack or a small candle holder and some matches. For a communal celebration only, you will also need one

10cm candle per person and one 12cm square of cooking foil per candle used. Fix the orange candle inside the cauldron or pot, either with the Blu-tack or by putting it into a small candle holder inside the cauldron. For each small candle, make a holder from a foil square. Place the candle upright in the centre of the foil. With your hand underneath, gather the centre of the foil around the base of the handle leaving enough of the foil to act as a guard for your hand to catch any dripping wax. Put the candles on a tray to hand round.

When you begin, the room should be dark, lit only by the altar candles and candles at the four quarters (page 16). Everyone stands round in a circle. If you can alternate male and female members round the circle, do so, but don't worry too much about this if there are children present who need to be next to their parents. Put the cauldron with the orange candle on the floor in the centre. Stand it on something heatproof if necessary. Pass round the small candles. If you are doing this as a solitary ritual, sit on the floor by the cauldron. Everyone stays quiet as a female member of the company says:

O gentle Goddess, mother of us all,

Give birth to your son,

Who will become your lover,

To bring fertility to the Earth and to our plans.

O Triple Goddess of the Circle of Rebirth,

Renew yourself,

That you will once again be young,

So you can run through the fields in spring

To meet your son and your lover.

Light the candle in the cauldron, then a male participant should say:

We rejoice for the birth of the returning Sun,

We rejoice for the Earth who welcomes his warmth,

Golden Sun,

Shine on the land and waken the world.

The woman replies:

> The circle of life is unbroken
>
> The Goddess is three in one,
>
> The wise crone, who led us through the dark,
>
> The mother with her new born son,
>
> And the daughter, born of herself, a twin to the son.
>
> Blessed be the Great Goddess who has created Life from Death.

The man says:

> Great God of the Sun,
>
> Of the day and night,
>
> We welcome your return.
>
> We look forward to the light that you will bring.
>
> May you shine brightly upon the earth and grow in strength.
>
> All blessings upon you.

Then everyone sings to the tune of 'The Holly Bears a Berry':

> *Now the Holly bears a berry, as milk it is white,*
>
> *And the Goddess bore the God Child on a Midwinter Night,*
>
> *And the Goddess bore the God Child the Green Man for to be,*
>
> *And the first tree in the Greenwood it was the Holly,*
>
> *Holly, Holly, and the first tree in the Greenwood it was the Holly.*

Then someone (their gender is not important) says:

> We will each light our candle from the new Sun's warmth.

Whoever lit the large candle, lights their small candle from it and then gives a light to the person on their left. The flame is then passed clockwise round the circle as someone says:

> As you light your candle,
>
> Think of the Sun shining on a new world.
>
> Make this world green and warm,

Happy, laughing and joyful.

Where there is no oppression,

Where everyone is free to be themselves,

Where everyone has enough

But never too much,

Where we can use our hands and minds creatively,

Where each person values his own talents,

And shares them skilfully and joyfully with others.

In the year to come,

Remember this world.

In your own way, however small, help to create it.

Notice how the light and warmth grow as the flame is passed around. Stay in silence for a few seconds when everyone's candle is alight.

ALTAR AND DECORATIONS

Use red candles and a red or red and green cloth and decorate it with sprigs of evergreen.

YULE INCENSE

2 teaspoons frankincense crystals

1 teaspoon myrrh crystals

1 teaspoon pine needles

½ teaspoon juniper berries

2 drops frankincense oil

CAKES AND WINE

Rich cake and mulled wine are traditional elements of the Yule season.

Rum cake

8oz/225g stoned dates

5fl oz/125ml rum

5fl oz/125ml red grape juice or orange juice

8oz/225g wholemeal flour

½ nutmeg, grated

1 teaspoon ground cinnamon

6oz/175g butter, softened

4 eggs, beaten

1 medium carrot, finely grated

6oz/175g sultanas

6oz/175g raisins

4oz/125g glace cherries

Chop the dates and soak them in the rum and fruit juice for twelve hours. Heat the oven to 300°F/160°C/Gas 2. Liquidise the dates, rum and juice in a food processor. Put in the flour, spices, butter and eggs and work everything to a smooth mixture. Turn the mixture into a bowl and fold in the carrot, sultanas, raisins and cherries. Put the mixture into a greased 30 x 25cm tin. Bake the cake for 45 minutes or until a skewer inserted into the centre comes out clean. It will cook to a very dark colour because of the dates. This does not mean that it is burned. Turn the cake onto a wire rack to cool. Cut it into small squares for use.

Mulled wine

1 bottle dry red wine (not too cheap)

3oz/90g honey (or more to taste)

2 7cm cinnamon sticks

2 pieces blade mace

1 chip nutmeg

1 small piece dried root ginger, bruised

1 small orange, sliced without peeling

1 apple, sliced without peeling

Put all the ingredients into an enamel or stainless steel saucepan. Set them on a low heat and bring the wine to just under boiling point. Keep it hot, but not boiling, for ten minutes and leave it in a warm place for a further 20 minutes. To keep the wine hot until the end of your ritual, put it into a flask and pour it out when needed.

THE PLAY OF THE HOLLY KING AND THE OAK KING

CHARACTERS
WISE WOMAN
WISE MAN
HOLLY KING
OAK KING
WREN
ROBIN
FATHER YULE

WISE WOMAN:
Pray, silence, my sisters and brothers,
And take heed to our play,
We've come to make a merry rhyme,
All on this Solstice Day.
Listen to us and you shall hear
The story of the wheel's turn,
So take your ease and listen,
While the Yule Log, it does burn.

WISE MAN:
There are two kings that rule the year,
Its waxing and its waning,
The Holly King for when the Sun goes down,

The Oak, to watch its gaining.
But don't just listen to what I say,
Walk in Oak King, and clear the way.

OAK KING:
In comes I, the Oak King,
From the other side of the year I came,
With my crown of leaves and acorns,
A king of greatest fame.
I watched over the year's waxing,
But since June in the ground I've lain,
And now I come this Solstice Night
To fight the Holly King again.
I saw the Holly King standing by,
I took an oath that he should die.
I'll cut him down all in his prime
And banish him away until another time.

WISE WOMAN (SINGS):
Holly, Holly,
And the first tree in the Greenwood it is the Holly.

HOLLY KING:
In comes I, the Holly King,
In the year's darkest time, of me they sing.
My berries red and leaves of green thorn
Give people hope on the darkest morn.
I reign through the waning of the year
And I'll fight that Oak King, if he be here.
His leaves are gone, his branches bare,
But my leaves shine in the frosty air.

Oak King, you cannot challenge me
The days are yet dark, my people agree.

OAK KING:

King Holly, your people long for the light,
They don't wish their days to be turned into night.
They need Sun to banish the frost and snow,
For trees to leaf and crops to grow.
My leaves may now be cast asunder
But my branches bear buds for summer splendour.
And now as ruler I must take my turn,
Put up your sword, and this lesson learn.

HOLLY KING:

I'll put up my sword to defend my throne,
And I'll fight well for the crown, before I'm done.

WISE MAN:

See how they fight long and hard for the crown,
But King Holly has won, the Oak King goes down.

WISE WOMAN:

No wonder it looks like King Holly has won,
For the people need cheering when the day's without Sun
They need his red berries and green thorns sharp
To garland their feast and shine in the dark.
But the wheel it must turn, the year must go round,
So I call on the Robin to heal this wound.

ROBIN:

In comes I, Robin of the wood,
I come to heal the Oak King, for the people's and the year's good.

WISE MAN:

How will you heal him, Robin?

ROBIN:

I'll pluck from my breast some feathers red,

The colour of blood, to raise the dead.

I'll lay them on his wound so deep,

Their magic will bring him round from his sleep.

ALL SING:

Now the Holly bears a berry, as blood it is red,

And the King of the Oak Tree he will rise from the dead,

And the King of the Oak Tree, the ruler he will be.

And the first tree in the Greenwood it was the Holly.

Holly, Holly,

And the first tree in the Greenwood it was the Holly.

WISE MAN:

And so the Oak King rises, tall and strong.

And once again, the battle is long.

But now the Holly King is down,

The Oak King has won the waxing year's crown.

WISE WOMAN:

But the people still need their Midwinter cheer,

They can't see the Oak's splendour at this time of the year.

They want shiny red berries and leaves that are green,

So I call on the wren, the Greenwood Queen.

WREN:

In comes I, the Wren so small.

The Holly is my master, so I come at your call.

WISE MAN:

Can you heal this King?

WREN:

I can heal him, so he will stay
And cheer all our hearts until the Twelfth Day.
Although Oak is the King, Holly's Lord of Misrule,
To gladden your hearts at this good feast of Yule.

WISE MAN:

How will you heal him?

WREN:

King Holly has a lady, the Ivy in her bower,
With jet black berries and sweet scented flower.
Her leaves are as green on the dark winter morn
As those of the Holly, but without any thorns.
When the Lady Ivy lays down by his side,
The Holly will rise and take her for bride.

WISE WOMAN:

Together they will grace our Midwinter Hall
Till on the Twelfth Day they will leave us all.

WISE MAN:

Then the days will lengthen again
And the Oak King truly begin his reign.
At Imbolc, when the green shoots rise,
The Holly will seem to go out of our lives.

WISE WOMAN:

But soon once more the wheel will turn,

And the old story again we'll learn.

ALL SING:

Now the Holly bears a berry as green as the grass

And the Sun it will grow stronger as the winter days pass

And the Sun it will grow stronger the springtime to foresee

And the first tree in the Greenwood it was the Holly.

Holly, Holly,

And the first tree in the Greenwood it was the Holly.

WISE WOMAN:

And now our story we have told,

A tale of wisdom for young and old.

From the parts we played let us be set free

And our own true selves we now shall be.

THE COMPLETE YULE RITUAL

Cast the circle and invoke the Goddess and God as on page 18. The ritual can be said by one person but it is best to share out the words so nobody dominates.

ONE PERSON SAYS:

Through the darkest of days

Nature has slept

And our souls have slept,

Nurturing the seeds of our new beginnings,

Waiting for the magical rebirth,

When the Sun's first rays

Bring warmth and light.

Now the Earth is dark,

The Earth is asleep.

With the coming of the Sun

She will gently awake.

The God has become Lord of the Shadows,

The Goddess is Wise Woman and Crone.

It is time for their rebirth,

It is time for their renewing.

Then use the ideas suggested earlier in this chapter to cover all the following activities:

- 'Waiting for the light' meditation – one person reads down to '….wonder if the sun will ever return to plant your seeds'.
- Welcoming back the Sun – after the cauldron has been lit, read the last part of the meditation and then continue with the rest of the meditation words until everyone's candle has been lit.
- The Holly King and the Oak King – to introduce the play, one person says: 'In the cycle of the year, it is now the time that the Holly King is slain by his brother the Oak King in the ancient story of death and rebirth.'
- Gifts – one person says:

Gifts at Yuletide are tokens of love and friendship,

They are symbols of sharing what we have with the world,

Of sharing our lives and hearts with those who need them,

Of our giving freely, expecting nothing in return.

FATHER YULE COMES IN WITH A SACK OF PRESENTS AND SAYS:

In comes I, old Father Yule,

Welcome in or welcome not,

I hope old Father Yule will never be forgot.

I fly with my reindeer, and have on my back,

All stuffed full of gifts, my magical sack.

My gifts are those of the present and past,

Gifts to be treasured and gifts that will last.

Those of the past are the lessons learned

From the year's experience, which cannot be spurned.

Those of the future are prophecy and truth,

And wisdom for all, not too much, just enough.

And when you receive them, think what you can give

To the world in return, for as long as you live.

Gifts are for giving, you must understand,

So share your new wisdom, hold someone's hand.

Use those gifts that have been given to you,

For the good of others the whole year through.

Sing for their pleasure, dance for their joy,

Or sit quiet and listen, and understanding employ.

Thank the Goddess and God at this time of our feast

For friendship and love and all of your gifts.

(*He gives out presents from his sack*.)

This is a time for plays and a time for jest,

A time for pleasure and a time for rest,

But now it is time for me to ride,

I wish all those gathered here a joyful Solstice Tide.

Now the holly bears a berry as black as the coal,
And we drink for our health from the deep wassail bowl,
And we drink for our health and the land's fertility
And the first tree in the Greenwood it was the Holly.
Holly, Holly,
And the first tree in the Greenwood it was the Holly.

- Cakes and wine
- Any other songs and stories that anyone present wishes to perform.

Blessing

The Solstice is:

Evergreen and Yule log,

Shining lights and decorated tree,

Wassail bowl and cake,

Acknowledgement of gifts

And joy in the returning Sun.

May the Goddess and God keep you safe and warm this Solstice tide

And in the lengthening days to come.

Close the circle (page 18).

CHAPTER 3

IMBOLC

Imbolc falls on 2 February. This early spring festival has been called Imbolc, Imbolg (both correctly pronounced without the 'b' sound) or, less often, Oimelc. The precise meaning of these variants is unknown, but it is thought that 'Oimelc' refers to 'ewe's milk' and that 'Imbolc' means 'in the belly', which refers to the quickening of the Earth as it prepares to produce the green shoots of spring (see Janet and Stewart Farrar's *Eight Sabbats for Witches*). The Christian festival, which occurs on the same day, is known as Candlemas. Pagans sometimes use this term as well.

THE FESTIVAL AND ITS MEANING

Imbolc is a gentle festival at which we celebrate the beginning of spring, the first stirrings of shoots in the Earth and the gradual dawning of the new light. We are back to work in earnest after Yule, but the dark days and winter weather are still very much in evidence. Imbolc is the glimmer of hope and promise. It is a time to clear out old habits and possessions, to discover the child within ourselves, make new beginnings and, most of all, honour the Goddess in her guise as Brighid (pronounced 'breed').

Imbolc is a time for getting ready for the new season. We finally clear away the evergreens of winter and ritually sweep the ground in preparation for new beginnings. We remember the seeds of our aspirations, now deep in the Earth, and imagine the first shoots pushing up towards the light and the roots getting stronger and reaching into the Earth for nourishment.

We honour the Goddess and God in their childlike aspects and seek the child within ourselves. Learning to play and laugh when the days are still cold and dark is a tonic to everyone. We also try to experience the wonder of childhood by looking at Nature as though for the first time. This helps us to appreciate the natural world around us so that we will care for it in the future.

We welcome the Goddess Brighid into our circle and recognise the gifts that she brings. From the God we learn that the world is full of new opportunities that are there for our use. He offers us the strength to make our projects grow.

Imbolc is what is known as a 'fire festival', but it is the returning light that we celebrate rather than the Sun itself. If you are an early riser, you will notice that each day the Sun rises a little earlier, giving us a few minutes more daylight. It is this light that stirs the seeds under the ground.

GODDESS AND GOD

At Imbolc, the Goddess is evident in all three aspects. She is the wise crone who now retreats into the shadows of winter, she is the quickening Earth, still nurturing her seeds underground, and she is the young girl, playful, laughing, gentle, leading us out towards the spring.

The names given to the Goddess at Imbolc are Brighid, Brigit, Bridget, Brid, Bridey and sometimes Brigante. I always use the first one, but it is really a matter of preference. They are all names for the same Goddess. She has been worshipped as such since the times of the early Celts and love for her was so strong that she became Christianised as St Bridget, sometimes called the 'Mother of all Ireland' and second saint

in importance there only to St Patrick. She had her own rituals, which were passed on to those of the Catholic faith in Ireland and Scotland and which were even preserved in a slightly different form in non-Catholic Wales. It was one of the few times of the year that the Christian Church, in these places at least, honoured and respected womanhood, the one time when the ancient Goddess reached out and touched people's hearts. Brighid is the Goddess of healing, poetry and craftsmanship, and of the hearth and home. She brings these gifts to everyone, male and female, and we call on Her to help us to make use of them.

The God is a young boy, confidently experiencing the world for the first time, exploring its opportunities and claiming it for his own.

Both Goddess and God are aware of each other as loving companions and playmates, who know that they are made for each other and that one day in the not too distant future they will lie together to experience the ecstasy of love.

OUT WITH THE OLD, IN WITH THE NEW

It is still wintertime. The doors and windows are shut, the curtains are drawn early and very little light has been reaching dusty corners. This applies not only to the physical world around us, but also to our minds. Now is the time to get ready for the Sun to shine in and to get rid of anything unwanted so that the new season can begin. First, think of old habits or aspects of yourself that are no longer relevant to what you wish to achieve. Make a mental note to discard them or perform the ritual below using old Yule greenery to help you. Likewise, try to clear your house of clutter – something easier to say than do, but really worth the effort.

GROWTH OF PROJECTS

Think back to Yule. Our future projects were seen as a bag of seeds. At some time after Yule, your seeds were planted. Now, the first rays of the

Sun warm the Earth and they start to grow. Keep this image to mind and use it to help you work towards the things that you wish to achieve. There is a short meditation and visualisation in the ritual below.

CHILDHOOD LESSONS

At Imbolc, the Goddess and God are imagined as growing children, setting out on a new life. There are certain aspects of childhood that are valuable and should not be forgotten, however old we are. Laughing, playing and discovering new things should feature in everybody's life. Another way of learning from childhood is to rediscover ourselves as we were when we first started out and consider how much we have lost and gained for good or bad. At Imbolc, we can rediscover parts of our personalities that we have forgotten and give thanks for what we have kept.

IMBOLC AND FOLK CUSTOMS

BRIGHID'S BED

The festival of the Goddess Brighid was probably Celtic in origin and the custom of making 'Brighid's Bed' survived into Christian times as the practice of welcoming in St Bridget. In the islands of Scotland and the Isle of Man it was carried on into the eighteenth century. Whatever form the welcoming took, in all places it was mostly carried out by the women of the family, the men only being allowed in later. The main part of the ritual was to prepare a bed for Brighid or Bridget and open the door and bid her welcome. The bed was, in different places, a cradle, a sheet, a specially prepared place on the floor, scattered rushes or a straw bed in a barn. The representation of Brighid was a decorated sheaf of oats, a corn dolly or an equal-armed woven cross. Sometimes there was no physical representation at all. In most places, the door of the house was opened and Brighid invited in. The doll or other

representation was put into the place prepared. Beside her was placed what has been referred to as a club or wand. The obvious explanation of this is that it was, at one time, a symbol of the God, but this aspect remains a mystery. What is known is that the club was a means of divination. If its print was discovered in the ashes of the hearth the next morning, a good harvest was predicted. When both were in place, the company would say something to the equivalent of 'Brighid is come, Brighid is welcome', often three times. Lighted candles were placed around or on either side of the 'bed' and were left burning all night. In some places the doll was processed around the village, and food or decorations for the doll were given by people who saw her. The women celebrated together and the men were let in afterwards to pay tribute to the Goddess or Saint.

Brighid crosses are still sold in Ireland and have become a symbol of good fortune and protection.

CANDLEMAS

February 2 became, for the Christian Church, the Feast of the Purification of the Virgin Mary and so its associations with the Goddess and womanhood were maintained. It also became the day on which new candles were taken to the Church to be blessed, hence the name, Candlemas.

In secular custom, it was recognised that the light was returning and a money-saving piece of country wisdom was:

On Candlemas day
Throw candle and candlestick all away.

Regulations for lighting the streets and engaging watchmen were relaxed with the gradual onset of longer days.

YULE DECORATIONS

The Christian festival of Candlemas became the last day on which to clear out the Christmas decorations. If any were left, they were supposed to bring bad luck and provide places in which goblins could lurk! We should now have left Yule behind and be looking forward to the coming year. Using the last remaining greenery in a clearing ritual helps us to do this.

THINGS TO DO

CLEAR OUT THE OLD

Do this on the night of Imbolc itself. If there are any aspects of yourself or any sorrows or bad experiences that need to be swept away with the

dust of winter, try this simple ritual using the old evergreens. You can work alone or within a group. You will need a few sprigs of the holly and ivy that have been saved from the Yule decorations (f you haven't kept any, make green paper leaves), a broom, and a paper bag, if you have no open fire. If you have an open fire, light it before you begin.

Cast a circle (page 17), then invoke the Goddess and God:
O great Goddess,
We call upon you as the young maiden
For whom the world is new and fresh.
We ask that we may act wisely
In clearing the way for our new beginnings.

O God of the Seasons,
We call upon you as the young boy
Discovering a new world.
We ask that we may act with strength
In clearing the way for our new beginnings.

Everyone takes a few leaves of holly and ivy. If you are working in a group, one person says:
Think of something in yourself that has to go.
Put all last year's mistakes behind you,
But take from them
A small piece of learning.
Forget the sorrows of the past,
But take from them
That small piece of light
Which all sorrows contain.
Sweep away the debris of winter.
Clear the ground for new beginnings.

If you are working alone, say:

> I need to let go of [state the things].
>
> I put all last year's mistakes behind me.

One person takes the broom and, starting from the north, sweeps anti-clockwise around the circle. As the circle is swept, everyone throws their leaves in front of the broom until they are all swept into a heap. This is then gathered up and either put onto the open fire or into the paper bag for burning later. If there is an open fire, say:

> As the fire burns away the things that are past,
>
> Mix your new learning
>
> Into this year's beginnings.
>
> Use it to make them grow.
>
> Mix the light-from-sorrow with the energy of the new season.
>
> Use it to make the energy strong.

If there is no fire, make the first line 'As the debris of winter is taken away...'. You may also like to repeat the chant when you finally burn the bag of leaves.

A female voice should then say:

> We thank the young Goddess of new beginnings,
>
> For her wise counsel.
>
> May we always listen to her in our hearts.

A male voice says:

> We thank the young God of the growing Sun
>
> For the strength that he gives us.
>
> May we always listen to him in our hearts.

Close your circle, and as soon as possible after the ritual, take the bag away and safely burn it in the garden or in another outdoor spot, making sure that you do no damage.

WELCOMING THE NEW LIGHT

This short ritual for Imbolc, ideal for performing after Clearing out the Old, can also be performed as a single unit. Work within a cast circle (page 17), either alone or with a group. Have ready a new, white candle in a holder or stand, preferably larger than an ordinary household candle, and a taper or matches. Put the white candle into the centre of the circle. One person says:

> Farewell to darkness, to unlit corners,
> The light steals in, the crone retreats.
> See the light at the edge of the shadows,
> Slowly it comes, the spring to greet.

Light the candle. Then the same person or another continues:

> This is the new light growing.
> May it burn brightly,
> For Brighid, the Goddess of new beginnings,
> And for the Horned God,
> Lord of strength and joy.
> Take a part of the light into yourself.
> May it warm you and lead you forward.

Or, if you are alone, the last two lines should be changed to:

> I take a part of the light into myself,
> That it may warm me and lead me forward.

A NEW WORLD

This is a visualisation for the first two weeks of February. Sit comfortably and make sure that you are not going to be disturbed.

Close your eyes, take three deep breaths and imagine a protective circle of blue light around you. Ask the Spirits of Earth, Air, Fire and Water to protect you on your journey. Call upon the Goddess and God to watch over you.

Imagine that you are in the dark cave of winter. The air is warm and musty. Imagine that you are gradually becoming a fox cub, with pointed nose and red fur. You are asleep, curled up with the rest of the litter against the warm body of your mother. In your dreams, you feel a fresh, tingly breeze waft past your nose, bringing with it the scent of green grass. You twitch your whiskers and begin to stretch. One by one, the others do the same. A ray of sunlight finds its way into your cave, showing up the dust of winter. You want to get out into the sunlight and the fresh, clean air. You have never been outside before. This will be the very first time. The whole of the outside world is completely new to you.

You approach the entrance to your cave with wonder and fascination. Look out. What do you see? A hillside? A valley? A field? Grass? Trees? Rocks? Look at them to see details such as the way the sun shines on them and the way shadows fall. What do you hear? Birdsong? Water? Wind? You have keen scent. What can you smell? Rain? Rabbits? Grass? Leaves on the path? Can you feel the wind in your fur? What is the ground like under your feet?

It is all so new. Experience it all for the first time. The dark cave of safety is still behind you but the whole new world beckons for the future. Sit and experience it for a while.

When you have done, turn back into yourself again. Gradually feel where you are. Feel the ground under you feet, the chair you are sitting on and come back to being you, today. Write your experiences in your Book of Shadows. Then, as soon as you can, go for a walk in a green space such as your garden, a park or the countryside. Remember how you felt when you were a fox cub, seeing the world for the first time. Experience that now. Look at the natural world around you as if for the

first time, savouring the sights, smells and feelings. You may think that, with the trees still bare and no flowers around, you wouldn't see very much, but look closely at that roadside verge, parkland grass or canal bank and see just how many small, green plants there are, waiting to grow and eventually blossom. Count how many different shaped leaves there are. This is the promise of Imbolc.

DO SOMETHING CHILDLIKE
Do this on Imbolc and during the two weeks after.

Everyone needs to play, to laugh and to forget for a time the general cares of everyday living. We need, in fact, to be children again. At this time of the year, when we think of the Goddess as a young girl, it is appropriate that we rediscover the child within ourselves and to feel, even for a short time, what it is to be 'care free'.

First of all sit with a group of friends and get each person in turn to mention one thing that they used to love doing when they were a child and that they don't do now. It is amazing just how much enthusiastic talk this generates and just how many things come up. Making dens, climbing trees, having pillow fights, making ice slides, lighting camp fires in the woods were just a few of the things that came up the first time that we tried this and many people just could not stop talking.

Next, give a bit of time to talk about just why we don't do this sort of thing any more and then find something that you can do and promise to go out and do it. Slide down a slide, lick a lolly, roll down a hill, run barefoot along a beach or go out to watch a children's film instead of the latest blockbuster. Whatever you choose, enjoy it, carry that enjoyment and sense of fun with you for the rest of the year and see if you can share it with others.

MAKING A BRIGHID'S CROSS
Brighid's cross was originally made out of rushes or straw, and it takes the form of an equal-armed cross with a woven centre. The one that I

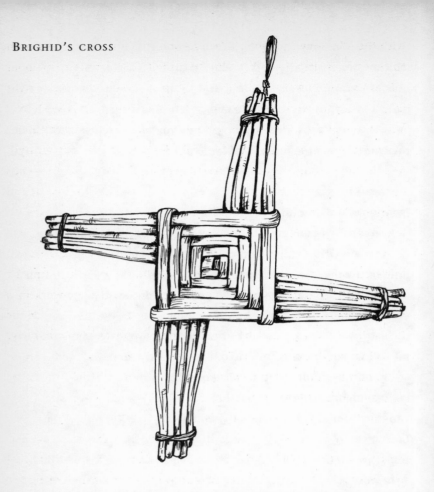

use was given to me years ago as a parting gift from an Irish family that we met while on holiday in West Cork. Some craft shops may sell them, but they could be difficult to find. If you can find rushes growing at this time of the year or if you are able to buy raffia or straw in a craft shop you can make one from these. You can also make a cross from something easily available – a sheet of white A4 paper. White is the colour of the festival, a clean colour for new beginnings. You will also need a small amount of liquid glue.

If using paper, cut it lengthways into 6mm wide strips. Take four strips of paper or straw and fold them in half crossways. Hold a strip

with the fold away from you. Take a second strip and loop it over both thicknesses of strip 1 about 1.5cm from the fold of strip 1 with about 1.5cm overlapping on the fold end. Strip 2 should now be at right angles to strip 1, with the fold on your left. Take strip 3, and loop it over strip 2 so that the fold is facing towards you and overlapping by about 1.5cm. Take strip 4, and loop it over strip 3, with the fold on your right and the tail pointing towards the overlap of strip 1. Push both free ends of strip 4 through the overhanging loop of strip 1. Lay the cross flat and gently pull the free ends of the strips so that the four make a cross with a neat woven square in the centre.

Now you know the structure of the cross, you can ease it apart again and secure the insides of the folds with glue. Once you have completed four interlinking arms, you can leave the cross as it is or work in a further four strips to make the cross double. These strips stay beside the first strips. As you are making or when you have made your cross, say:

As I weave this cross of Brighid,

To new beginnings let me take heed.

Leaving unwanted past behind,

A brand new world so let me find.

This cross is the symbol of your new beginnings. Write one thing that you would really like to achieve on each arm. These can be related to the tasks and meditations above. Pin the cross up where you can see it and let it stay in place until Ostara. Then keep it safe and burn it at Imbolc next year, along with the old Yule greenery.

THE CALL OF BRIGHID

Sometimes we are reluctant to come out of our cave, get rid of old thoughts and old possessions and start afresh, but Brighid's call is strong. The tune for this Imbolc song is the traditional tune 'The Keys of Canterbury'. It is best sung by at least two people as call and response, with a female voice singing the part of the Goddess and

either male or female, or a group of people, singing the response.

O won't you come with me along the way to seasons new

And share in all my pleasures and find a path that's true.

O will you come outside

And leave your past behind

And follow on with me to the spring.

O I won't come with you along the way to seasons new

And share in all your pleasures and find a path that's true.

I'm safely here indoors

With objects of my past,

And winter's cold it still stalks the year.

O I will show to you the way to write your words in rhyme

And sing of months and seasons and dance your steps in time.

If you will come outside, etc.

I do not wish to learn the way to write my words in rhyme

And sing of months and seasons and dance my steps in time.

I'm safely here indoors, etc.

I can guide your hand and eye to learn a craftsman's skill,

And from all natures colours create pictures at your will,

If you will come outside, etc.

O, I have not the hand and eye, etc.

O I can help you how to choose from every healing art,

So in this world of trouble, you can play your part.

If you will come outside, etc.

O I'm not worthy, etc.

O I can show you how to laugh and play just like a child,
And how to find your freedom and catch the spirit wild.
If you will come outside, etc.

O I'm too old to learn to, etc.

O I can lead you to the place that is your heart's desire,
You'll be healer, child and artist and tender of my fire.
If you will come outside, etc.

O, Goddess, lead me to the place that is my heart's desire,
I'll be healer, child and artist and tender of your fire.
O I will come outside
And leave my past behind,
And follow on with you to the spring.

THE BRIGHID DOLL

This is following the ancient Hebridean or Irish custom of making and decorating a straw doll in honour of the Goddess. It is a good way to welcome her into your heart.

You will need a bundle of garden raffia (you can buy this from ironmongers and garden centres, usually done up in bundles of about 3oz/80g); small, thin pieces of bright, shiny ribbon; small glittery things or natural things such as pieces of ear-rings and jewelry, small shells with holes in, even small holy stones.

Open out the bundle of raffia and lay it lengthways. Trim one end to make the pieces even. Measure up 60cm from the trimmed end and cut right across the bundle. Take up, as one piece, all the 60cm lengths of raffia and fold them in half. Tie one strand of raffia tightly 10cm away from the fold to make the 'head'. You will find that, once you have done this, the bottom part will fan out beautifully, like a skirt. That is the basic doll.

The Brighid doll can hang in your house for the duration of the festival, until Ostara or until Imbolc next year, when you make a new one.

PINE CONE WAND

This is used in the Ritual for Brighid, below. We take it to be a symbol of the God and the promise of his coming together with the Goddess at Beltane. If you cannot get one made, just use a stick, about 22cm long and 1.5cm in diameter. You will also need a pine cone, a long kitchen matchstick and some wood glue.

With a bradawl or fine drill, bore a hole in the base of the pine cone to fit the width of the match. Bore a similar hole in the top of the stick to a depth of about 2.5cm. Cut the top off the match. Coat one end with glue and push it into the pine cone. Cut the remaining length of the match to fit the hole in the stick. Coat it with glue. Push the stick onto the match. Leave the wand for the glue to set. Once made, you can use it year after year.

RITUAL FOR BRIGHID

This is a welcoming ritual for the young Goddess, based on the Irish and Hebridean custom of making a doll from a sheaf of oats and welcoming her into the house. You can do this alone or with others. The custom was originally carried out only by the women of the house,

PINE CONE WAND

but this does not have to be so now. Welcome both sexes into the circle but, just for this time, allow the women to play the main parts.

Make a Brighid doll as above. Lay a white cloth in a wicker basket for Brighid's bed. If you have no basket, use a shoebox covered with a plain or flowered wrapping paper. Have ready two new white candles in holders and a taper or matches for lighting.

One person holds the doll on the edge of the circle, standing at the East to represent the sunrise. If you are doing this alone, leave the doll in the East. The 'bed' is placed in the centre of the circle, with the candles on either side. Light the candles. (If you are doing this as a part of a longer ritual as set out below, place the bed in front of the newly lit white candle.) One person goes to the East and says:

The bed is ready.

Brighid, Bridgit, Briganti,

Brid, Berta, Bridey,

Spring Goddess since the world began,

Goddess of light and sun,

Giver of warmth and health,

In winter's cold, we call to you.

The person holding the doll takes two steps towards the centre of the circle and says:

The Goddess Brighid has come to your circle.

She is the giver of the healing arts,

Of creativity and craftsmanship,

And of the love and wonder of life

That comes with childhood.

She brings a promise of summer sun

And the joy of loving.

Pay heed to the gifts that she brings

And use them wisely.

The doll is carried around the circle for everyone to welcome. As this is done, each person in the circle adds one or more decorations. (The Hebridean custom was to place a special jewel on her heart.) If you are performing this ritual alone, sit in the centre of your circle as you attach the decorations. When the doll is ready, she is taken to the bed and placed in it. All say three times:

Brighid is come. Brighid is welcome.

Lay the wand or pine cone stick beside her. Leave the bed as it is overnight, but blow out the candles before you go to bed in the interests of safety.

Altar and decorations

Use white candles and decorate the altar with white flowers. You should be able to find one or two snowdrops in the garden at Imbolc, but I prefer to leave them where they look best and buy flowers instead. If you have room and like making a display, you could also add quartz crystals and white stones and anything white or transparent and sparkly.

Have vases of white flowers around the house.

Imbolc incense

2 teaspoons myrrh

1 teaspoon dried rosemary

1 teaspoon juniper berries, crushed

¼ teaspoon dried thyme

2 drops lemon balm oil

2 drops sandalwood oil

2 drops sweet orange oil

Milk and dairy products are the significant foods for Imbolc, so make a rich soda bread with soured cream and flavour warm milk with honey and brandy.

Soured cream and honey cake

8oz/225g wholemeal flour

1teaspoon bicarbonate soda

½ teaspoon salt

½ teaspoon ground cinnamon

2oz/50g butter

3oz/75g raisins

5fl oz/125ml soured cream

3oz/100g honey

Heat the oven to 400°F/200°C/Gas 6. Put the flour into a bowl with the bicarbonate of soda, salt and cinnamon. Rub in the butter with your fingertips. Toss in the raisins. Make a well in the centre. Pour in the soured cream and add the honey. Gradually mix everything to a dough. On a floured baking sheet, roll the dough into a square about 2cm thick. Bake the cake for 12–15 minutes, or until it is firm and slightly browned on top. Lift it onto a wire rack to cool. Cut it into small squares for serving.

Brandied milk and honey

15 fl oz/375ml full cream milk

3oz/75g honey

3fl oz/75ml brandy

Put the milk and honey into a saucepan and stir it over a low heat so that the honey dissolves. Bring to just below boiling point. Take the pan from the heat and stir in the brandy.

This must be served hot, so if your ritual is to be a long one, put the milk and honey into a vacuum flask, keep it near the altar and pour it into your chalice when it is needed.

THE COMPLETE IMBOLC RITUAL

Cast the circle and invoke the Goddess and God as described on page 00. A female voice says:

Half way between Solstice and Equinox,

The Goddess is here in her triple aspect.

The young Goddess, Brighid, walks through the dark, cold land.

She brings the first stirrings of Spring.

As she passes, she brings new warmth and new light.

Mother Earth is quickening.

Soon she will bring forth new life.

Leaves will uncurl, shoots push upwards.

The world will be green again.

The Dark Crone, in her wisdom,

Retreats to the shadows,

To wait for her time to come round again

But she leaves behind some of her wisdom

That it may be used in our new beginnings.

Then a male voice says:

At Imbolc, the God is a young boy,

Adventurous, inquisitive,

Looking at the world with new eyes,

Knowing that all opportunities are open

And that he can make all endeavours successful.

With courage, he goes forward into the new season.

Another voice (male or female) says:

> We have spent the long days of winter in the dark cave of the Earth Mother. Now it is time to stretch ourselves, to shake off the dust and go out like a young fox cub into the sunlight, to explore the world.

Then use the ideas suggested earlier in this chapter to cover all the following activities:

- Welcoming the new light
- Ritual for Brighid
- Prayer for new beginnings – hold hands in the circle and imagine a cone of light in the centre, as one person says:

> We send out a cone of power.
> In the name of the young Goddess and young God.
> Let us think of new beginnings,
> With harm to none and for the good of all.
> The first for the World.
> The second for a person known to us.

If you have a Tibetan bowl, ring it now while everyone concentrates.

> And now new beginnings for ourselves.
> At Samhain, the seeds of our new ideas were only dreams.
> At Yule, the seeds were illuminated by the Sun.
> On Twelfth Night, we planted them.
> Now, at Imbolc, it is time for growth.
> Close your eyes and imagine.
> Deep in the earth lie the seeds of your desires
> Named for your projects or changes in life.
> Your seeds have shoots.
> They are beginning to push upwards towards the Sun.

They are beginning to send down roots into the Earth.

With the energy of the young Goddess,

The seeds of our new ideas will grow in strength.

With the care of the Mother,

We will nurture them.

With the wisdom of the Crone,

We will put them into practice wisely.

And with the strength of the Horned God,

We will have the courage to see them through.

Brighid, Bridgit, Brigante,

Goddess of new beginnings,

Of creativity, poetry and craft,

Of healing, hearth and home,

We call to you, that this may come to be.

- Making Brighid's crosses – in the circle, all make crosses together and all say the chant together when they are made. If there are a lot of people, it is probably best to do without the glue at this point as it will take too long. Leave the glue for after the circle has been closed.
- Song: 'The Call of Brighid'. After the song, one person says:

  Know and remember that Brighid is always with you.

  You carry her magic in your heart and mind.

  Call on Brighid as you work.

  She will bring you the inspiration that you need.

- Honouring childhood – go round the circle with everyone making a contribution.
- Cakes and wine.

Blessing

Imbolc is:

New light

New beginnings

Birdsong and snowdrops

The stirring of seeds

The first shoots of green growth

It is:

Time to put plans into practice

Time to make thoughts into activity

Time to make creativity real.

May your seeds grow strong and your plans come to fruition,

And may you enjoy the growing light.

Blessed be.

Remove the bed and candles (still alight) to somewhere safe for the rest of the evening, then close the circle. At the end of the evening, put the bed back into the centre of the room, without the candles, and leave it there overnight.

CHAPTER 4

OSTARA

Ostara falls between 20 and 23 March, depending on the movements of the Sun. Consult an astrological chart or diary for the precise date.

The name is that of the Anglo-Saxon Goddess of the Spring, which has been spelled Eostre, Eostra, Oestara and Ostara, and is probably a western variant of the eastern Goddesses Astarte, Ishtar and Aset. Ostara is the Latinised version which I use simply because I like it best and so as not to confuse it with the Christian festival of Easter, to which the Spring Goddess gave her name. The festival is also often referred to as the Spring or Vernal Equinox.

THE FESTIVAL AND ITS MEANING

Ostara marks the point in spring when the hours of light and dark are equal and so it is a good time in which to balance the things we do in our lives. From now on, the daylight will gradually overcome the darkness, enabling our dreams and projects to grow. We see them as the first green shoots pushing up towards the growing light or as new life, breaking out of the egg of winter.

The Earth begins to really wake up at Ostara and nature is young and fresh like a child. Even on dull days, the light is more intense and you can feel the first excitement of spring in the air. Birds are mating and nesting and yellow flowers reflect the growing Sun. New life, green shoots and spring flowers are celebrated as the gifts of the Goddess and

God. We repay the joy that they bring through working for the Earth's protection and by sharing our gifts and caring for others.

Ostara is a time for exploring the countryside and for planting seeds and working in the garden. On wild and windy days, seek the Ostara Hare who brings not only eggs, but freedom and courage. On warm days, bask in the Sun like the snake to recharge your health and energy. Never pass over the chance to be young at heart so, at a time when the Goddess and God are still young and playful, climb a tall hill to roll eggs and enjoy being childlike again.

GODDESS AND GOD

In the story of the Wheel of the Year, the Goddess and God are young and just beginning to come to sexual maturity. They look upon each other with love and longing and dance together in the spring Sun. Their desire can be seen in the rising sap in the trees and the pushing up of green shoots. The young Goddess has even given her name to words such as oestrous and oestrogen, which we associate with female sexuality in both animals and humans. She carries with her the egg, symbol of fertility and new life and is accompanied by a hare.

There are many legends to explain the Goddess's association with the hare. One that is supposed to be Viking in origin tells how, one bitterly cold March day, a young girl out collecting fire-wood found a small bird almost frozen to death. The girl, unable to do anything herself, called on the Goddess for help. The Goddess answered and walked down a rainbow to the Earth, melting the snows, bringing the sunlight and causing lilies to spring up and flower wherever she went. Because the bird's wings were frozen and it could no longer fly, the Goddess turned it into a white hare, which laid rainbow-coloured eggs. She told the girl that the hare coming to the woods every year would signal the beginning of spring. Eostra's hare may have become the

'Easter Bunny', but he still brings his gifts of eggs in the spring!

Another symbol of the Goddess that we recognise at this time of the year is the snake, which comes out of hibernation in March to bask in the growing Sun, warm its cold blood and soak up the energy. Because it sheds its skin, the snake was an ancient symbol of new life coming out of old. A snake coiled in a circle with its tail in its mouth symbolised everlasting life and a snake wrapped around an egg was called the 'World Egg', laid by the snake as symbol of the Goddess. Every spring, the serpent helped the world to hatch out from this egg.

OSTARA AND FOLK CUSTOMS

The customs and traditions that are associated with Ostara are mainly connected with eggs and new growth and these have been taken over by the Christian Easter. Any other customs and rituals remaining that may once have been associated with the Equinox itself have been lost in the mists of time, but we can reclaim the ones that we know about.

EGGS

Eggs have come to be the symbol of the Christian Easter but, as we have seen in the legend above, their association with Ostara and new life is far, far older. Eggs have featured in countless creation myths since time began and the World Egg, swimming in a primal sea, was said to have hatched the Earth. Eggs, to primitive peoples, were something of a mystery. The outside that was so smooth, so strong and so still, suddenly produced a new, irregular-shaped baby animal or bird. The yolk of the egg to some peoples, symbolised the Sun, so an egg in the spring symbolised the returning of the Sun to the Earth. Eggs have symbolised fertility, resurrection and re-birth. They have also been given as a sacrifice to the returning Sun, in place of a human sacrifice, and eggs were buried in the Earth to give back their life-giving properties and ensure a good

harvest. The Druids revered the egg and wore, as a badge of office, an egg-shaped red stone or fossil around their necks, which was called the 'glain' or sea serpent egg. Because of this, eggs did not feature in their diet.

Much later, the Christian Church forbade the eating of eggs, dairy products and meat during Lent (the 40 days before Easter) with the result that, as chickens start to come into full lay at this time of the year, many households experienced a glut of eggs even though they were living on dried beans and salt fish. There were therefore plenty to spare when the fast was lifted and various games were invented that became a part of the seasonal celebrations. Egg rolling consisted of rolling hard-boiled eggs down a hill to see whose went furthest and lasted the longest. In the game of egg shackling, the cooked eggs were shaken in a blanket and again the longest-lasting was the winner.

In the twentieth century, chocolate eggs became more and more available and Easter egg hunts became popular.

THINGS TO DO

EMERGING FROM THE EGG

Do this on the night of Ostara. Emerging from an egg is a good symbolism for starting to put our plans into practice. Within your circle, either specially cast or as part of a longer ritual, have an egg in a dish or in an attractive egg cup. Hard boil it first, in case of disasters! Hold up the egg and say:

Spirits of Air, Fire, Water and Earth,

Share the secrets of this sign of rebirth.

Lord and Lady of the Spring

You've guarded its truth since time began.

All through the winter it has been the sign

Of safety, protection and waiting our time,

Nurturing the embryo plans and dreams

Till we feel the warmth of the Sun's beams.
We give thanks for nurture and fertility
But, now to progress, we need to break free.

The same person or another, continues:
Our plans have been nurtured in the egg of our dreams.
Now they are ready to take on life of their own
In the warmth and energy from the growing Sun,
We/I call into action the 'egg-tooth', that small amount of effort
That it takes to put our/my plans into action.
Plans must be let out, or they may never grow.

Use the following meditation, either as a speech by one of a group, or simply as instructions if you are working alone.

Imagine an egg that contains symbols for the projects that you wish to put into practice this spring. Within the egg is also a large, golden yolk. As you watch the egg, visualise the yolk getting gradually smaller and the symbols growing larger, so large that they take up all the space in the egg. They cannot grow any more and they cannot get out. Above the egg a small speck of golden light begins to grow. When it is larger than the egg, it sends down a beam of light to warm it. The egg begins to glow in the light. A crack appears around the circumference and the two halves burst apart. Your projects fly up into the light and begin to grow again. Name them and recognise them and promise yourself to allow this growth to continue.

CREATING YOUR OWN PROTECTIVE EGG

Besides being something from which we need to break out, eggs can also become our protection, a small haven into which we can retreat whenever we need comfort or peace. You can create this small piece of protective space in your own mind and use it whenever you feel the need. You can do this at any time of the year, but the Spring Equinox,

when we are already thinking about different kinds of eggs, is a good time to set it up. This is not a new or original idea, but something very useful which many people do to ease tensions and stress.

Find a place where you will not be interrupted. Take three deep breaths and call upon the protection of the Elements and of the Goddess and God. In your mind, create an egg of blue light around yourself. Sit and feel it all around you. Outside the blue egg, create a shell. It is thin but strong. It will let the light in and lets you see out, but it will keep the cares of the world on the outside. The inside of the egg is your own space which is always comfortable and welcoming. Nothing can penetrate it. Whenever you feel the stresses of life are getting too much or if you feel you are being attacked in some way, simply imagine that you are going into your egg. After a short while, you will be able to do this anywhere, even when there are people around you. In fact it is sometimes to deal with these people that you call it up. It is your protection and will deflect anger or aggression away from you. When you have no need of it any more, imagine yourself calmly stepping out of it feeling relaxed and comfortable. One thing you must not do, though, is stay in it all the time. You don't want to retreat from the world for no good reason, only to keep stress at bay when necessary.

EGG ROLLING

One day between Ostara and Easter, we go up onto the Downs to roll eggs. We spend some time the night before hard-boiling and decorating them in a number of ways. Felt-tipped pens, acrylic or watercolour paints, marker pens and even nail varnish are all called into use for the purpose and the eggs are transformed into faces, snakes, flowers or simply a skyscape of stars. One egg was all black and another simply had 'EGG' written on it in large letters. These are just some of the more memorable ones and every year they are different. We make a day of it, take a picnic and also some small prizes (chocolate eggs of course) for the winners. We have heats for different age groups and a grand play-off at the end.

The way people look at this activity differs. Many just treat it as a good day out but, because of something that happened the first time I rolled eggs, I tend to regard it as a pleasurable way of making a sacrifice or a gift to the Earth. I had made an egg which I was really, really pleased with. I had drawn a black spiral around it, filled it in with green and black zig-zags, given it a head and forked tongue and it became a snake. After being rolled down countless times, it did not want to break, so I took it home. I left it in a box, but then what? I couldn't leave it to go rotten in the house. I also felt rather guilty about bringing it back. So it landed on the compost heap, given back to the Earth at last. Now, no matter how much I like my egg, I always make sure that it breaks on the hill. The egg, and the effort that I put into making it, is the gift and the sacrifice to thank the Earth for its bounty. Think about this as your egg rolls down the hill.

Another way is to write a promise on your egg that will help the Earth in some way. Make it something that you know you can and will carry out, for example recycling your rubbish, planting a tree or giving to an ecological charity.

Never worry about leaving the broken eggs on the hill. Overnight, foxes and other wild animals will come and eat them. Pupils from a local school usually roll their eggs down the same hill a few days before us and, by the time we get there, all that is left are one or two small pieces of shell.

FLOWER RITUAL

Do this on Ostara night or at any time when you have an abundance of spring flowers. Spring flowers, often yellow, always bloom to brighten dull March days. Main roads into towns are lined with huge beds of daffodils. Out in the country there are dandelions, celandines and primroses reflecting the growing Sun in various shades. Light green and yellow are the colours of the spring and of the young God and Goddess, and spring flowers are symbols of their blessing on the emerging season.

Flowers always tend to bring out the best in people and the mere fact that there is a vase of them in a room seems to be therapeutic. This simple flower ritual is based on this idea. Use daffodils which are grown and picked specially for putting into vases and leave the wild flowers to decorate the countryside. You can use the ritual on its own or combine it with others.

Cast your circle, then hold up the flowers in the centre of the circle. Say:

These are the flowers of spring,

Young, fresh and innocent as a new born child,

Symbols of the beauty of life.

Wherever flowers grow,

May they bring joy,

And the inspiration to care for others.

Go to the East and say:

I/We call upon the Spirits of the Air to bless these spring flowers, so that the memory of them will inspire us to always think the best of other people and never to look for the worst.

Go to the South and say:

I/We call upon the Spirits of Fire to bless these spring flowers, so that their memory will inspire us to go out and actively help people in need.

Go to the West and say:

I/We call upon the Spirits of Water to bless these spring flowers, so that the memory of them will inspire us to seek ways in which we can help and heal other people.

Go to the North and say:

I/We call upon the Spirits of Earth to bless these spring flowers, so

that the memory of them will inspire us to strive to make people happier in the world.

Hold up the flowers in the centre again and say:

These flowers are the gifts of the Goddess and God. May they inspire us to recognise the Goddess and God in all human beings. So mote it be.

RENEWING ENERGY: A VISUALISATION

Do this at Ostara or during the week after. Throughout the cold months, cold-blooded animals hibernate. Their body temperature drops to a degree that can just sustain life but no more. They conserve energy by going into a state which is deeper than sleep until the growing strength of the Sun gradually draws them back into a wakeful state. In order to gain the energy to move, eat and mate, snakes must bask in the Sun in the spring, drawing in the warmth that will raise their body temperatures. At Ostara, it may well be too cold for us to lie in the Sun but, through visualisation, we can still gain relaxation, health and energy from its light.

Sit down somewhere comfortable, close your eyes, take three deep breaths and relax your body from the feet upwards. Imagine you are a hibernating snake, in a dark hole. You are cold and are curled up, deep in sleep, with no energy to move your body. Gradually, you feel the air around you become warmer. It gives you just enough energy to slowly crawl out onto the short grass of a sunny hillside. Experience the Sun. It is a golden light above your head. Feel its warmth flood through your body, from your head downwards. Each time you breathe in, this golden light floods further down. As you breathe out, it intensifies. When your whole body is filled with light, bask in it and enjoy it. You are sunbathing on this grassy hill. Tell yourself that the Sun's golden power is bringing you energy and health after the long winter. Believe it.

When you are ready, gradually begin to become aware of where you are sitting and of your feet on the ground. Slowly open your eyes. Even if it is cold and raining outside, maintain the feeling of light and warmth within you and remember it whenever you feel low. Write about your experiences in your Book of Shadows.

EARTH HEALING

This can be done any time from Ostara to late April. This is a ritual that we did in a local forest on Earth Healing Day (April 19) some years ago, when the area was under threat from developers. It also fits in well as a part of the Ostara ritual, to protect the new, young world as it begins to grow. Although it was originally intended to be used outdoors, a few minor adaptations make it suitable for using inside.

You will need a feather, a red flower, a small amount of water and a small stone. These are all things that, if left in the countryside, soon become absorbed into it, doing no damage and causing no litter.

One person may do the talking or separate people can call on each element. If you are outside, stand around a tree. If you are inside, stand in a circle. Cast the circle (see page 17) if you are performing this as a single item, and not as part of a larger ritual. The person says:

May the Lady be with us as Lady of the Forest.

May the Lord be with us as Lord of the Wild Wood.

As Pagans, we are dedicated to the healing of the Earth. We must call upon the guardian Spirits of Air, Fire, Water and Earth to help us in our task.

Take the feather to the East, hold it up and say:

O Guardian Spirits of the Air, who are the medium of vibration and the breath of Life, blow gently on the Earth. Blow away any negative powers, leaving love and peace in their place.

Leave the feather at the East point of the circle. Take the red flower to

the South, hold it up and say:

O Guardian Spirits of Fire, who bring warmth and comfort to our lives, let your warmth soak into the Earth so the seeds will grow, flowers blossom and the trees unfold their leaves. Burn away any negative powers, leaving love and joy in their place.

Leave the flower at the South point of the circle. Take the water to the West, hold it up and say:

O Guardian Spirits of Water, who are in the soft summer rains and the waves of the oceans, wash the Earth clean. Heal her with your crystal springs and cleanse the land with your rivers. Wash away any negative powers, leaving love and healing in their place.

If you are outdoors, pour the water on the ground at the West point of the circle. If you are indoors, leave it in its container. Take the stone to the North, hold it up and say:

O Guardian Spirits of the Earth, who watch over the wild places, the forests and woodlands, and who know the secrets of healing and growth, teach the people of the Earth to respect the gifts of nature. Disperse in your depths any negative powers, leaving love and harmony in their place.

Leave the stone at the North point of the circle. One person says:

May we work with the Spirits of the Elements to preserve the beauty of all the Earth.

If you are worried about any particular place that is under threat, make a special plea for it here. As an example, this is what we used for the local forest. Adapt it as you need. (The 'mounted army' was once seen with the 'inner eye' many years ago by someone who had been walking in the forest on a cold November day, so we called upon them as special spirits of the place.)

This forest is in danger from those who, for greed and for profit, will cut down its trees, not seeing their beauty and knowing nothing of their power. We now call upon the special spirits of this place, who once revealed themselves as a mounted army, and offer our healing and positive thoughts, that they may act as a protection to prevent or lessen the evil that may threaten.

If you are outside, hold hands around the tree. One person says:

We take this one tree as a representative of all the trees in the forest and send to it a circle of healing and protection.

Instead of 'forest' you could also say 'world' if you are not concentrating on any one specific place. If you are inside, just hold hands and say:

We send out a light of healing and protection to all wild places [or to a specific named place].

Dance a spiral dance (see page 156) around the tree, visualising the power that you raise going out to help this tree and all trees everywhere. If you are indoors, dance around the room. A really good song to sing during this ritual is the chorus of the song 'Tread Gently' by Carolyn Hillyer from her album *House of the Weavers,* produced in 1992.

Touch the ground to 'earth' any excess power, then close the circle. If you have been working indoors, take the feather, flower, stone and the water to an outside place and leave them where they will do no damage.

Soon after we had carried out our ritual in the forest, a whole group of Pagans and eco-warriors took up residence in the forest and continued and very much magnified the work that we had begun. At the time of writing, five years later, no development has yet taken place.

THE GIFTS OF THE HARE

The hare, probably because of its old association with the Goddess, was once a witch symbol, and it was thought that, when in danger, a witch

could turn herself into a hare and so outwit her persecutors or pursuers. Hares are free spirits, running wild in the country with just a dent in the grass for a home. They are also very bold – my husband once saw one run down the middle of our village street in broad daylight on a Sunday morning.

Look at a picture of a hare and read about its habits and habitat. Think on the gifts of the Ostara Hare and take them into your life.

- Courage and boldness: be brave in your choices and strong in your convictions. Walking the Wiccan path may not always be easy. We need to be sure in our beliefs and brave enough to stick by them.
- Freedom: be a free thinker. Don't let advertisements get to you and don't buy things, wear things or do things just because everyone else does. Make your own choices.
- Wildness: go out in the March winds into a wild landscape and just enjoy it.
- Love of the Goddess: in some legends, it is the hare's love of the Goddess that makes him bring the coloured eggs in her honour. Give your gift of love to the Goddess and remember to thank her for the many gifts that she gives to you.

Hare in the wind,
No one shall you bind.
Hare in the rain,
You never seek gain.
Hare in the Sun,
Outwitting the gun.
Hare in the night,
You love the Moon's light.
Hare of the Goddess at this turn of the year
Share with us your wildness and lack of all fear.
So mote it be.

Trying something new

Because there is a bright new world out there, go out any time during the two weeks after Ostara and find something new to do unconnected with anything that you take part in at the moment. This is not as easy as it sounds because the threads of our lives are connected in many different ways, but it is an exciting proposition and could be the beginning of the realisation of dreams or a whole new lifestyle.

Altar and decorations

Have a bright green or pale yellow cloth and light yellow candles. Decorate it with spring flowers, mainly daffodils. Put vases of spring flowers around the room.

Cakes and wine

Ostara biscuits

These were once traditionally baked at Easter time all over England. They are rich, buttery and fruity.

4oz/125g wholemeal flour

4oz/125g butter

½ teaspoon ground cinnamon

½ teaspoon ground mixed spice

2oz/50g currants

1oz/25g chopped mixed peel

4oz/125g soft brown sugar

juice ½ lemon

1 egg

1 tablespoon milk or brandy

Heat the oven to 300°F/180°C/Gas 4. Put the flour and spices into a bowl and rub in the butter. With your hands, mix in the currants, peel and sugar. Make a well in the centre. Beat together the lemon juice, egg

and brandy and pour them into the well. Mix everything to a stiff dough and knead it lightly. Roll the dough to a thickness of about 6mm. Stamp it into rounds with a 6–7cm biscuit cutter. Lay the rounds on a floured baking sheet. Bake them for 20 minutes, or until they are firm and beginning to brown. Lift them onto a wire rack to cool.

Lemon, honey and barley water
This is a pure, fresh, non-alcoholic drink to give health and zest for the new season. There is more here than you will need, but the rest can be enjoyed on another day.

2oz/50g pearl barley
3 lemons
2½ pints/1.4 litres water
2oz/50g honey

Put the pearl barley into a saucepan with the water. Bring it to the boil, cover and simmer for 20 minutes. Meanwhile, grate the rinds from the lemons into a large jug or bowl. Cut away and discard all the white pith from the lemons. Thinly slice the flesh and add it to the grated rind. Strain the hot liquid from the barley over the lemons and lemon rind. Stir in the honey. Leave the drink until it is completely cold and pour it into your chalice straight from the jug, without straining.

COMPLETE OSTARA RITUAL

You will need a candle in a cauldron or holder; a vase of daffodils; feather, stone, red flower and water; a hard-boiled egg in a bowl or egg cup; a bowl of small chocolate eggs (one for each person plus one over).

Draw the circle and invoke the Goddess and God, as on page 18. The song that runs through this ritual is to the old French tune of 'Love Will Come Again'. It can also be spoken.

Light and dark are equal,
The Sun is gaining power,
Green shoots are growing,
Buds come into flower,
Goddess and God
Dance through the fields in play.
Life comes to the Earth
So rejoice in the lengthening day.

Now the sap is rising,
Now the brown soil is turned,
Feel the Earth's vibrations
As the Spring returns.
Take winter's dust
And cast it all away.
Life comes to the Earth
So rejoice in the lengthening day.

One person says:
>   We made plans in the winter,
>   We sowed seeds,
>   We had dreams.
>   Now our plans will come to be,
>   The seeds of our ideas will grow,
>   Our dreams will come true,
>   The light will come
>   Out of the dark of winter.

One person lights the candle in the cauldron and says:
>   We light this candle symbol of the growing Sun,
>   In honour of the Goddess as Spring Maiden

And of the young God.
May the flame be a flame of love
That we send out
To all the world.

One person says:

Around the candle's golden light,
We raise the power this magic night.

All hold hands in a circle and dance or move clockwise around the candle. One or all sing the third verse of the song as you go round. Sing it at least twice:

Light the flame of love
And dance round it in a ring.
Send out its power
To make the whole world sing.
Send joy, peace and laughter
To light where all is grey.
Life comes to the earth
So rejoice in the lengthening day.

Stop. Close your eyes and imagine a golden cone of light that you can send out to do good in the world. A Tibetan bowl can be rung if you have one. One person says:

Send out the power.
Let it heal a laughter-starved world.
Let it take joy and peace and hope
To every dark corner of minds and hearts and lives.

One person sings the fourth verse of the song:

Raise the flowers for blessing,
Take them round the ring,

Gift of the God and Goddess,
Symbols of the spring.
We seek to give joy,
May the flowers show the way.
Life comes to the Earth
So rejoice in the lengthening day.

Then use the ideas suggested earlier in this chapter to cover all the following activities:

- Flower ritual
- Earth healing, after which one person sings the fifth verse of the song:

    We have kept within us
    The sleeping egg of life.
    Let the Sun's bright rays
    Crack it open like a knife.
    From the shell of Winter
    Comes a bright new day.
    Life comes to the earth
    So rejoice in the lengthening day.

- Emerging from the egg
- The gifts of the hare. One person holds up the bowl of chocolate eggs and says:

    The Hare's eggs are a sign that spring has truly begun. May we grow and progress as the season grows and enjoy the gifts of the Hare.

Distribute the eggs, but don't eat them yet. The next day, unwrap the remaining one and give it back to the earth, along with the cakes and wine.

One person sings the final verse of the song:

> *Shake off all care*
> *And run to greet the Sun,*
> *See the bursting buds*
> *Whose life has just begun,*
> *Run wild with the hare,*
> *And walk the ancient ways.*
> *Life comes to the Earth*
> *So rejoice in the lengthening day.*

- Cakes and wine

Blessing

Ostara is:

New light;

Soft, sweet air;

The running Hare and spring flowers;

The bursting of buds;

And the straight following of new paths.

May the Spirits of the Air guide our thoughts when we set out on new paths.

May the Spirits of the Sun and Fire give us vitality and passion to make new ventures successful.

May the Spirits of Water help us to tread new paths with balanced emotions.

May the Spirits of the Earth give us physical balance so we may draw life and health from the strengthening Sun.

May the Goddess and God watch over us this springtime and may we continually remember to give thanks to them for this new season.

So mote it be.

Close the circle.

CHAPTER 5

BELTANE

Beltane is always on 30 April and celebrations can last well into the night and often extend, with or without a break, until the morning (and sometimes into the day!) of 1 May.

Beltane, pronounced exactly as it is written, is the Anglicised name of the festival, which is the most simple to use. The Irish version is Bealtaine and the Scots Bealtuinn or Bhealtyainn, both pronounced with a *by* sound at the beginning and an emphasis on the final *n*. There have been many Sun Gods with names such as Beli, Belios, Balor, Bel, Belios and Belenos, which can all probably be traced back to the biblical god Baal, whose name translates simply as 'Lord'. It is therefore probable, but by no means proven, that Beltane has acquired its name from this source. Another theory is that it comes from a Celtic word meaning 'bright fire', a reference to the bonfires that have always been lit on May Eve.

THE FESTIVAL AND ITS MEANING

Beltane celebrates the beginning of summer. It is a time of music, dance, song and the enjoyment of nature. Sexual love, creativity, fertility and fire are its themes. Suddenly the countryside is a thousand different shades of green, the dawn chorus loudly greets the day, the blackthorn (if not the hawthorn) shows white in the hedges, clouds of bluebells colour woodland floors, and stitchwort and columbine star roadside verges. It sounds clichéd, but it is true. No wonder that in folklore and song May has always been described as 'the merry month'. In the television series *Robin of Sherwood*, when Robin Hood first meets Marian he tells her: 'You look like a May morning'. For thousands of years, May has signalled the end of winter's hardships. Animals were once driven out to their summer pastures at Beltane, green shoots of the crops began to grow steadily, and warmth and light had returned.

We celebrate the Earth's fertility and our own creativity. We try to make sure that our projects and opportunities are growing strongly. As the God and Goddess create life, so we look to our own creativity to bring our projects to fruition. It is also a time to rediscover the love that we have for our respective partners as the Goddess and the God rediscover one another. We stay up late, get up early, light a fire, make a Jack-in-the-Green (see page 123) and dance round it and sing traditional and newly written May songs. We go out into the streets and dance to carry the message of the returning summer to everyone we meet. Beltane is never a serious festival, although, as always, we take its message to heart.

GODDESS AND GOD

In the story of the year's wheel, the night of Beltane is the most exciting and the most sensuous. The Goddess and God are youthful and strong and ready for their first experience of sensual pleasure. On Beltane night, they come together and lie with each other for the first time. There is the thrill of first meeting, the excitement of the chase, the falling in love and the joyous coming together in the Greenwood. Their sexual union ensures the fertility of the earth, the fertility of our minds and the pregnancy of the Goddess who, in the depth of winter, will give birth to the God once again. The song 'May Eve' (page 138) celebrates this story.

CREATIVITY

The atmosphere of live excitement that you can feel in the air around Beltane can be channelled to help you both to work on creative projects and to work on projects creatively. This doesn't just mean writing a poem or painting a picture; it could also mean approaching work problems in a creative way. The two visualisations below will help you to channel your own creativity.

FERTILITY

May is the time when the fertility of the Earth is tangible. Bare plots become green and flowers and fruit trees blossom. In the story of the year, we celebrate the sexual fertility of the Goddess and God, which ancient agricultural people believed would ensure the fertility of the family, the tribe, the land and the flocks and herds.

The sexual union of the Goddess and God ensures the pregnancy of the Goddess so that the Wheel may turn again. While we celebrate our own creativity and go forward with this year's projects, we must also be aware of the small seeds of ideas that come into our mind for the things that we would like to achieve next year. Let them fall into fertile soil so that we can continue our progress.

BELTANE AND FOLK CUSTOMS

The festival of Beltane, or May Day as it is more often called, is associated with numerous folk traditions. Their origins are lost in the distant past and whether or not they are Pagan cannot be proved, but I don't think that it matters. All I know is that the traditions, songs and dances help to make Beltane what it is: a joyful and truly enjoyable celebration.

Throughout the Medieval period, May Day customs were tolerated by the Church and they became an established folk tradition, enjoyed on a rare day's holiday by a large proportion of the population and sometimes even used to raise money for the Church. Whether they were thought to have any association with the old Pagan religion is unknown, but May games, Maypoles and Morris dancing, the plays of Robin Hood and going out into the woods all night with your chosen partner, survived into Tudor times. The Protestant Tudors frowned on May customs, and Oliver Cromwell banned them (he also banned Christmas). Some of the traditions failed to be revived with the Restoration (1660), but the basic message of celebrating the first day of summer was far too ingrained in the psyche of many people to be abandoned altogether. In the eighteenth century, chimney sweeps still took round their Jack-in-the-Greens (elaborate guises of greenery swathed over willow withies), Maypole dancing was re-introduced with additional ribbons as a pretty Victorian children's pastime and one or two customs survived without a break. Two world wars nearly destroyed the lot, but along came the folk revival of the 1960s. Now, it is all out there for you to find. There are traditional songs and place to use or adapt, and customs old, new and revived taking place all over the country for everyone to go out and enjoy. May Day is alive and well and growing.

BELTANE FIRE

Fires, blazing on the hilltops, were once the focal point of Celtic Beltane celebrations. They symbolised the return of the Sun bringing fertility and plenty to the Earth.

The fire was called the 'need-fire', or *tein-eigin*, meaning that it was essential to life. The central fire in the living accommodation meant warmth and cooked food and it was kept burning all the year. At Beltane, all the fires in a settlement or village were put out and a new, communal Beltane fire was lit from a large piece of oak by using friction. Everyone took a piece of this fire to re-kindle their own hearth. It was a wonderful way of sharing, starting afresh and establishing a feeling of one-ness within the tribe.

When the need-fire died down, couples wanting children leapt the

flames together and pregnant women did so to ensure an easy delivery. Good fortune, safe journeys and the successful completion of ventures were wished for in the same way. The next morning, when the ashes were cool, flocks and herds were driven over them for health, fertility and good milk yields. Blacking your face with the ashes was also thought to be lucky and, if everyone did it together, it was another way of encouraging unity within the group.

CAKES AND SACRIFICE

It is a distinct probability that Beltane celebrations of thousands of years ago involved a human sacrifice, given in return for the coming of life to the Earth. How it was done is unknown, but it is probable that the person was chosen by means of drawing lots. A flat cake, like an oatcake, was baked on a hot stone, broken into pieces and offered around. The person who took the most blackened part, was the sacrifice. In *The Golden Bough*, James Frazer describes similar customs, although without the sacrifice, surviving in Scotland and Wales as late as the eighteenth century. The taking of the oatcake was the same, but the 'sacrifice' was merely a pretence of throwing the 'victim' on the Beltane fire or an order to jump the flames.

I have known some covens make a cake for Beltane and actually colour a single portion black with food colouring. The person who gets it knows they have a lesson to learn in the coming year. I personally don't agree with this. It can worry the recipient and destroy for them what should be a joyful festival.

Instead, I make a version of 'flapjacks' for the Cakes and Wine ritual and cook them until the top begins to go uniformly dark. Then everybody gets a piece of dark and light to remind them that there are joys to be had and lessons to be learned. (Now for a confession: the first time I did this, it happened by accident as the oven was too hot and I made a joke of it, but everyone thought it was a good idea!)

The other cake that is a feature of Beltane, is the rich fruit cake that

you will sometimes see impaled on a sword, being carried round by Morris dancers on May Day morning and being distributed amongst the dancers and onlookers. This is something I have seen done (and done myself) over the past 30 years or so, but so far I have found no written reference to its significance. Some Morris sides do it because it is part of their tradition, but they don't know the reason why. Recent word of mouth folklore says that it symbolises killing winter, represented by the dried fruits and nuts, in preparation for the fresh foods that summer will provide. Whatever the reason for doing it, it's great fun and adds to the celebrations on May Day morning.

SUMMER KING AND WINTER KING

There is a legend that, on Beltane night, two Kings fight for the hand of the Queen. After many hours, the Summer King triumphs and rules the land for the next six months. The Queen, or Earth Goddess, knows the outcome and knows that they are really two aspects of the same person and she joyfully accepts the victor as her consort.

GREENWOOD MARRIAGES

In the days when we lived much closer to the Earth, Greenwood marriages were accepted as part of May Day custom. Young unmarried people chose a partner and rushed off to the woods to spend the night making love under the stars, thus celebrating and re-enacting the union of the Goddess and God and ensuring the continuation of the tribe. Even after Christianity came, the custom carried on, gradually dying out towards the sixteenth century. This may not be considered appropriate today, but Beltane is a time for enjoying and celebrating sexual love with your partner and re-affirming your commitment.

BRINGING HOME THE MAY

On the way back from the Greenwood, in the early morning, the revellers brought back branches of flowering May blossom and

sometimes went round the village begging for gifts in return. However, because of the calendar change in 1752, when twelve days were removed so we could come into line with other countries, you will rarely find May blossom on May Day today. Make a flower garland instead.

MAYPOLE, MORRIS AND DANCING UP THE SUN

Dancing in some form or another is another important feature of May Day morning. The original Maypole is said to have been a phallic symbol, representing the God and with the crown of flowers surrounding the top representing the Goddess. Dancing round it celebrated their union and the fertility of the Earth. Or did it? Again, no one really knows. What we do know is that ribbons did not feature in the early days and that the custom was banned by Oliver Cromwell. However, by the eighteenth century it was once more widespread. Ribbons were introduced in the nineteenth century when Maypole dancing lost most of its communal significance and became something that was taught to children.

Start talking about Morris dancing and Paganism and you step into a minefield! There are Morris dancers who are Pagans and Morris dancers who are definitely not. Some care passionately about whether the two are associated and some do not! Again, nobody knows the truth and it shouldn't really matter. We all celebrate May Day in our different ways and watching Morris dancing is another way of enjoying the festival. A lot of Morris sides dance at sunrise, more because it is a tradition than because of their beliefs. May Day is the first day of the dancing year and can be celebrated for that alone.

JACK-IN-THE-GREEN

This is another custom of unknown origin. For the people I celebrate with, this eight foot high frame of greenery has become the symbol of the returning summer, a direct descendant of the Green Man of the

Woods and a representation of the mature God. For the chimney sweeps who paraded with him during the eighteenth and nineteenth centuries, he was an excellent means of collecting money for their annual feast! Whatever he means to you, enjoy him. Jack-in-the-Green parades can be found at Rochester and Hastings.

The May Morning dew

Washing your face in the May Morning dew is said to make you beautiful. Running barefoot through the dew is said to keep you healthy for a year. There's no harm in trying.

THINGS TO DO

Listen to your heart

There is always a point, in the week coming up to Beltane, when you walk outside and suddenly feel the 'zing' and excitement of anticipation in the air. Once this has happened, it can be very hard to concentrate on anything. At Yule, there is a calm stillness. Before Mayday, it's as though everything is waiting to explode. Channelling your creativity (see below) is one way of dealing with this, but you also need to take time just to enjoy yourself. In Britain the first Monday in May is a Bank Holiday, so go out and enjoy it. Forget the decorating and the household chores, and treat the day as everyone once treated May Day. Use it for enjoying the outdoors and Bank Holiday activities, for dancing and laughing and just generally having a good time.

Sometimes, however, this isn't enough. Most years, you can go back to work feeling refreshed and happy after this brief fling, but what about when work has become something to dread going back to? In Barry Unsworth's novel *Morality Play*, which is about a band of Medieval strolling players, the main character is a priest who has run away from his secretarial duties three times, '...and always at the

Maytime of the year at the stirring of the blood'. The story is about the last time he does so and his final decision, made in the middle of winter, is to stay with the players and give up being a priest altogether.

I'm not suggesting that at Beltane everyone turns in their job and goes off back-packing round the world, but it is worth paying heed to this restlessness and making the first steps towards improving your lot. Deep inside, do you know that what you are doing is no longer for you? If so, take time to really think about why this is. Can you do something to improve your job, or your attitude towards it? If not, consider changing it. Then think about whether you want a similar job with a different employer or whether you want a complete change. Whichever the answer, take steps towards making this happen. Talk to colleagues, look in the jobs section of different publications, make enquiries about training schemes or courses that will give you the right qualifications for a complete change. You don't have to jump in with both feet straight away, but it is worth putting wheels in motion. Even considering something carefully can alter what happens to you.

You may then, like Unsworth's priest, come to the conclusion that: 'The impulse to run away had not been folly, but the wisdom of my heart.'

CHANNELLING CREATIVITY

This visualisation can be done during the week coming up to Beltane and the three weeks after. Any project on which you are working around the time of Beltane will always benefit from the creative excitement and energy that characterises the festival. What needs to be done is to channel it, otherwise your mind may jump about like Tigger, spread the energy too wide and waste it.

This visualisation is best done, in the morning, preferably when the Sun is shining. It is an excellent visualisation to do outside but, if you can't find anywhere that feels safe from intrusion, it is best to work in a safe place indoors, with the windows open. If you intend to work outside, find yourself somewhere to sit where you won't be disturbed.

This could be in the garden, by the seashore, in the woods, on a hill, by a country track, anywhere where you feel comfortable and safe. If you are indoors, unplug the phone.

Think of a creative project that you are working on and would like to see through in the best way possible. It could be anything at all, large or small, connected with work or leisure – it is up to you. Close your eyes, take three deep breaths and imagine a protective 'egg' of blue light around yourself. Inside your head, call in turn on the Spirits of the Air, Fire, Water and Earth to protect you by saying:

> I call upon the Spirits of Air to protect me in my quest and to gently blow the creative energies of Beltane towards my goal. I call upon the Spirits of Fire to protect me in my quest and to help me to find the strength and determination to see my project through. I call upon the Spirits of Water to protect me in my quest and to send their cool waters to clear my mind and bring concentration. I call upon the Spirits of Earth to protect me in my quest and to ensure my feet stay on the path towards completion of my task.

Then call upon the Goddess and God:

> I call upon the Goddess and God as Creators of Life, that the task I set out to do be in their honour and for the good of all.

Name or describe your project and say:

> This is what I wish to see successfully completed, in the name of the Goddess and God, with harm to none and for the good of all.

Imagine you are in a deep woodland, walking down a path through the trees. The path is wide enough for you to comfortably walk down without brushing branches on either side. The leaves are bright green, fresh and new. The forest floor is firm and brown under your feet. You can see that the Sun is shining above the trees. You can hear a stream

flowing nearby and smell the scent of the woodland. A gentle breeze rustles the leaves. The light is vibrant and you gradually see that it is made up of thousands of tiny golden grains, jumping and swirling in the air, creating a golden mist. Look through the mist to the end of the path, which may still be quite a long way away. The trees come to an end there, and there is a clearing. In the clearing see an image of the project that you are now working on as you wish it to be when it is finished. Put your arms out to the sides, palms facing forwards. (If you are completely alone, you can do this for real if it helps, if not, just imagine it.) Bring them slowly forwards, parallel with your shoulders, palms facing towards each other, and, as you do so, bring a portion of the golden energy from the sides to the front of you so it is held between your hands. It glows brightly. Using the power of your mind, send this golden light along the path ahead of you, not too fast and not too slow. Direct it into the image of your completed project, which then becomes clear of mist. This is your creative energy being focused. Now resolve to follow it along the path, keeping the clear image of the project in your mind. Then say:

I thank the Spirits of Air for their protection.

I thank the Spirits of Fire for their protection.

I thank the Spirits of Water for their protection.

I thank the Spirits of Earth for their protection.

I thank the Goddess and God and honour them in my heart.

Become aware of your surroundings and of yourself and gradually open your eyes to the outside world. Over the time that it takes to see your project through, think of that clear image whenever you need to.

THE BELTANE FIRE

Lighting a fire is a significant part of the Beltane ritual. We usually have a candle in the cauldron to use in the ritual and then light a fire nearby that burns as the ritual is in progress and is just low enough for jumping after the circle has been closed.

Lighting the cauldron candle

You will need a cauldron or heavy metal pot, a new yellow or gold candle, Blu-tack or a small candle holder and a taper. The ritual opens with a female voice saying:

> The Goddess is the cauldron. The candle is the fire of the God.
> Lord of the Greenwood, come to the Goddess, to bring summer
> back to the Earth.

A male member of the company lights the taper from the right-hand altar candle and uses it to light the cauldron candle. He says:

> I am the spirit of the Greenwood.
> I am the fire in your passion.
> I am the warmth of the Sun.
> I am the endurance of the stone.
> I am the strength in your heart.
> I am the greening of the leaves.
> I am the God who brings life to the earth.
> I come to my Lady.

A female voice replies:

> I am the spirit of the dance.
> I am the inspiration of the song.
> I am the colours of the rainbow.
> I am the beams of the Moon.
> I am the waves of the ocean.
> I am the weaver of the web of Life.
> I welcome my Lord.

Taking the need-fire

Each person will need a wide-necked glass jar, such as a 1lb/450g honey jar, approximately 1 metre of string, a nightlight and a taper. It is a good idea for the jars to be prepared beforehand with one or two spares in case

anyone unexpected turns up. With the string, make a handle on the neck of the jar. Wrap the string round the neck of the jar twice, leaving one short end and one long end of string. Tie the ends together securely in two or more knots. Take the long end of the string and pass it directly across the diameter of the jar. Tuck it through the string that binds the neck of the jar and make the part of the string that goes over the top of the jar the right length for a comfortable handle. Tie one knot directly opposite the first knot, and then pass the string over to the first knot, making the loop match the length of the first one. Pass the end of the string through the string that goes around the neck of the jar beside the first knot. Tie more knots to make it secure and cut off any long end which is left over. Put a nightlight inside each jar. Before the ritual begins, give each person a jar. Everyone stands round in a circle, and one person says:

> Before the Beltane fire was lit, everyone put out the fires in their own houses, even the hearth fire, the heart of the household, that never went out at any other time. All fires were then re-lit from embers of the sacred fire. From the candle (or fire) take a part of the flame and light your own fire.

Each person in turn lights their nightlight, either from the candle in the cauldron or from a bonfire. One person says:

> Remember this fire. Take it into your hearts. May it warm you and heal you and light your creative spirit for the rest of the year.

Weaving fire dance
This follows on from lighting the nightlights. It looks spectacular in a large space outside. Inside, it can be a bit of a squash, so clear the furniture before you begin and take care. One person with a good sense of rhythm will need a drum or anything else that you can beat a rhythm with, such as two flints or the rhythm sticks that you find on school percussion trolleys. Make the rhythm as simple or as complicated as you would like and keep it to a fairly fast walking pace.

All stand round, alternately male and female if possible (but don't worry if your gathering has a larger proportion of one sex), holding your lighted nightlights. The drummer stands in the middle. Turn to face someone else so one person is facing clockwise and the other anti-clockwise. If there is an odd number of people, the drummer must get into the circle as well. One person says:

We celebrate the coming together of the Goddess and God.

Together in love, may they bring

Truth and happiness to the world,

A return to the Greenwood,

An awareness of Nature,

The end of the destruction of the Earth and its peoples,

And the fulfilling of all wishes for the good of the Earth.

Weave a dance of sacred fire to bring this into being.

The dance is like a 'grand chain'. You pass the person you are facing by the right shoulder, and the next person you meet by the left, then right, then left, and so on all the way round and, if it feels right, round again. Hold your 'fire' carefully as you go. Walk to the rhythm of the drum and stop when the drummer stops.

Jumping the Beltane fire

Only do this outside. If you are working inside, see 'Circling the fire' below. The fire doesn't have to be large, it need not burn for a long time, and its nature depends on where you are celebrating. If you have a garden and have a particular place where you always have a bonfire, then light it there. The ideal place for me is the part of my vegetable patch that I am reserving for courgette and tomato plants that haven't yet been planted out. When the fire is out, I simply dig the ashes into the earth. You can make a fire-pit in a lawn by folding back turf from a small area (about 40cm square). If the turfs are replaced as soon as the ashes are cold, after a few weeks, you will not know they have ever been disturbed.

If you only have a patio, use a small, low, portable barbecue. Failing all this, a candle in a cauldron can be jumped over just as well. Place the candle in a lantern first, to stop it going out. Don't make it too high.

If you are working outside in the countryside, unless you have the landowner's permission to light a fire, use the candle in the cauldron. If you have the owner's permission, make a fire-pit, keep it small and make sure that it is all covered over when you have finished. Fires can destroy habitats and make unsightly scars. As Pagans, we are obliged to protect the countryside and not destroy it, so enjoy your fire but leave all as you found it.

As with all fires, always observe safety precautions. Make sure you have an extinguisher handy and watch out for children. Jumping the fire is an enjoyable custom but again you need care. Wear stout shoes and wait until the flames are very low. Watch out for long skirts or other trailing bits of clothing.

As you jump, make a wish for the coming summer, which can be for yourself, another person or the world in general, always for good and with harm to none. If you jump with a partner, you each wish the same thing, usually for the continuing success of your relationship. Another way is for everyone present to make the same wish, such as for the protection of the earth or for the healing of a friend, and as they jump they voice the wish: 'I make this jump for ...' Should you decide to jump with another person who is not your present partner, never take lightly who you jump with. I have seen more than one relationship (usually successful) begin with a casual jumping of the Beltane fire! Everyone circles clockwise around the fire chanting the following rhyme:

Fire to welcome ancient Gods,
Fire to greet the Sun,
Burning as we make our dance,
Jumping one by one.

Fire, burn this Beltane night,

Make wishes come alive.
Bring to us a summer bright
Let the Greenwood thrive.

Fire, give us warmth and light
All the summer through,
Burning as we make our dance,
Jumping two by two.

Fire, burn this Beltane night,
Make wishes come alive.
Bring to us a summer bright
Let the Greenwood thrive.

On 'Jumping one by one', one person leaps, and 'two by two' is the line for couples. Carry on until everyone who wants to has had a go. It may take a bit of organisation but will certainly bring great hilarity. Don't worry if not all goes to plan, the important thing is that everyone gets a jump who wants to, with whom they want to and that all is accomplished safely.

Circling the fire
Jumping the fire is too dangerous if you are working inside. However, there is no need to miss out completely. Hold hands around the fire and circle round it, chanting the rhyme. Instead of saying 'Jumping one by one' say 'Circle one by one'. Instead of jumping, the person or two people whose turn it is, makes a small clockwise circle of the fire inside the large circle. This can take place within the cast circle before taking the need-fire.

THE SUMMER KING AND WINTER KING
This is the old legend of Robin Hood as the Summer King, meeting Sir Guy of Guisborne, the Winter King. Marian is not the usual helpless

captive maid to be fought over, but the Lady who rules all, who sees the two fighters as two halves of the same man and who gladly acknowledges that his face changes with the seasons.

Characters

PUCK, A WOODLAND SPIRIT

MARIAN, LADY OF THE WOOD AND QUEEN OF THE SEASONS

ROBIN HOOD, THE SUMMER KING

GUY OF GUISBORNE, THE WINTER KING

ALL SING (TO THE TUNE OF THE KEEPER):
O, gather round now, if you would,
And come with us to the Merry Greenwood,
And we'll tell you the tale of Robin Hood,
Among the leaves so green-o.
Summertime,
Winter,
Wintertime,
Summer,
Leaves grow,
Leaves fall,
So it must go on,
Among the leaves so green-o.

PUCK:
Well met, my masters, and give room for our play,
We've come to tell you a story
On the eve of this May Day.
We have come to tell to you
The tale of an age-long battle,
How a Summer King and a Winter King
Do make their swords to rattle.

Now you've all heard tell of Robin Hood
With his bow and comrades bold,
But there is another player
Whose story must be told.
Robin Hood is the Summer King
(So I've heard from men of wisdom),
And the King who rules the Wintertime,
Is that knight, Sir Guy of Guisborne.
Never-ending is their fight
And each rules half the year.
But there is a gracious Lady
Who rules constantly here.

MARIAN:
In comes I, Marian,
Of all seasons I am Queen.
I reign in the grey of Winter
And in the Summer's green.
I am Queen of the sparkling stars
And Goddess of the Earth,
Giver of Life and bringer of Death
In the circle of rebirth.
There is one who rules with me
All the twelvemonth round,
But twice a year he changes face
And does battle for the crown

GUY OF GUISBORNE:
In comes I the valiant ruler,
Guy of Guisborne is my name.
With my sword and buckler by my side
I'm sure to win the game.

All through the dark of winter
I have held my sway,
And I intend to keep the crown
As April turns into May.

MARIAN:
My poor Sir Guy, he grows too old,
And summer approaches fast,
His other aspect now comes in,
His time will soon be past.

ROBIN HOOD:
In comes I, bold Robin Hood
With my bow of yew tree wood.
My arrows sharp I have to hand
To fight the Winter King for his land.
We are well met, Sir Guy,
You King of Winter grey,
For the Summer Kingdom now we must fight
From dawn till the end of day.

GUY OF GUISBORNE:
For to fight with me, bold Robin,
I fear you are not able.
For with my trusty broadsword
I soon will thee disable.

ROBIN HOOD:
Disable! Disable! It lies not in thy power,
For with my trusty broadsword,
I soon will thee devour.
Stand back, Guisborne, and let no more be said,

For if I draw my glittering sword,

I'm sure to break thine head.

GUY OF GUISBORNE:

Break my head!

How can'st thou break my head?

My head is made of iron,

And my body is made of steel,

My hands and feet of knuckle bone,

I challenge you to field!

PUCK:

And so they step into the ring,

And battle for the crown,

The swords sweep wide, the blood flows down,

And the King of Summer is first on the ground.

There he lies in the presence of us all,

On the Queen of the Forest now I must call.

MARIAN:

Well fought, Sir Guy, and bravely struck,

Winter King, who is held so dear,

But 'tis not the right time, you must fight again.

And go with the turning year.

I have a flagon of magic water,

To challenge your intended slaughter.

A drop to the head, a drop to the heart,

Rise up, Robin, and play thy part.

ROBIN:

And now, Sir Guy, we must fight again,

To see who is the best of men.

GUY OF GUISBORNE:

I count myself as good as thee.

ROBIN:

And so do I, as good as thee.

PUCK:

So they are, but one must die,

And on the forest floor must lie.

They fight again, till the Sun drops down,

And Guisborne is knocked upon the ground.

MARIAN:

Well they fought with equal might,

The result is true, the outcome is right.

ROBIN:

I think, my lady, that I have won,

And with my victory comes the Sun.

I've banished winter for many a day

And now it is the first of May.

PUCK:

Guisborne lies on the forest floor,

And summer is come again.

But all things go in circles, in truth,

And he will rise up from his pain.

Rise up, Sir Guy, and give me thy hand,

And forget your quarrels all.

For winter it will come again

When the leaves they start to fall.

ALL SING:

Summertime,

Winter,

Wintertime,

Summer,

Leaves grow,

Leaves fall.

So it must go on

Among the leaves so green-o.

MAY EVE: A SONG TO SING AT BELTANE

(The tune is the folk song, 'She Moved Through the Fair'.)

O, Lord of the Greenwood, we await your return,
And your Lady is waiting as the Beltane fires burn.
She dances in shadows, she hides in the trees,
She is there in the darkness where nobody sees.

And first she turns into a hare in the field,
And though you run after, she never will yield.
You can hunt her through hedges, through brakes and through briars,
But you never will catch her and she never will tire.

And next she turns into a doe in the wood,
And there you would find her if only you could.
She's white as the moonlight, but as wind she is swift,
And she leaps the wide river and the high hanging cliff.

When you've hunted the forest and all over the land,
You step into a green grove and there she does stand,
With her arms out to welcome and a smile in her eye
For her Lord of the Greenwood; and with you she will lie.

And the summer will come to our land once again,

Bringing birdsong and flowers and ripening grain.

So rejoice in each other till the dawn brings the light.

O Green Lord and Green Lady, we bid you 'Good Night'.

CAKES AND WINE

Ingredients in the cakes include oatmeal from the Celtic hearth cakes baked to choose the sacrifice, nuts for their sexual symbolism and honey for the honeymoon. Mead is the honeymoon drink. It is difficult to make from scratch, so buy it and then spice it to make it special.

Honey-nut flapjacks

4oz/125g soft brown sugar

4oz/125g butter, plus extra for greasing

2tbsp honey

8oz/225g porridge oats

3oz/100g chopped mixed nuts (these can be bought in a packet)

Heat the oven to 350°F/180°C/Gas 4. Put the sugar, butter and honey into a saucepan and melt them together on a low heat, stirring occasionally. Take the pan from the heat and stir in the oats and nuts. Put the mixture into a shallow ovenproof tin, about 25 x 20cm. Bake for ten to 15 minutes or until the top becomes flecked with darker brown. The mixture will still be soft. While it is hot, cut it into small squares. Leave the cakes until they are cool and firm. Transfer them to a plate.

Spiced mead

1 bottle (26fl oz/700ml) mead

10fl oz/300ml apple juice

12 cloves

1 cinnamon stick

2tbsp brandy (optional)

Pour the mead and apple juice into a saucepan. Add the cloves and cinnamon stick. Set them on a low heat and bring them to just below boiling point. Take the pan from the heat and leave the mead to cool completely. Strain it before use and add brandy if you wish.

BELTANE INCENSE

3 teaspoons frankincense crystals

2 teaspoons dried rose petals

1 teaspoon dried lavender flowers

1 teaspoon sanderswood

2 drops jasmine oil

2 drops neroli oil

2 drops sandalwood oil

THE COMPLETE BELTANE RITUAL

Cast the circle, and invoke the Goddess and God as on page 18. As usual, the words can be spoken by one person or be shared around the company, as you think fit. One person says:

Now is the time of flowers,

The time of the growing warmth of the Sun,

The time to dance and the time to love.

Now is the time of Beltane.

A female voice says:

We welcome the maiden Goddess who fills our hearts with love

And gives beauty and flowers to the world.

She comes as the stream and the cup to be filled,

She comes as the child who grows wise in the Sun,

She comes as the Moon who rises to full,

She comes as the Goddess who waits for her God.

A male voice says:

> The young God rises as the sap from the ground,
>
> He comes as the Sun to bring warmth to the Earth,
>
> He comes as the leaves to bring green to the world,
>
> He comes as the stag to give life to the herd
>
> He comes as the God who lies with his Lady.
>
> We welcome him.

> The Goddess is the cauldron. The candle is the fire of the God.
>
> Come to the Goddess, Oak King, that the Earth may be fruitful

Then use the ideas suggested earlier in this chapter to cover all the following activities:

- Lighting the candle in the cauldron
- Play of the Summer King And Winter King
- Song: May Eve
- Circling the fire (although if you have a separate bonfire outside, this can be done after the ritual instead)
- Taking the need-fire and the weaving fire dance
- Visualisation for channelling creativity. One person says:

> From the union of the Goddess and God
>
> Are created the fruits of the Earth,
>
> The harvest of grain,
>
> The hare in the corn,
>
> The deer in the forest.
>
> On this night, celebrate your own creativity.
>
> Think of one creative thing that you would like to do
>
> And hold it deep down inside you.
>
> Feel it folded like a leaf waiting for the Sun.
>
> Look at the glow from the fire in the cauldron.

Let the glow touch your leaf,

Let the leaf open to the Sun.

This is the leaf of your creativity.

Allow it to grow strong and sturdy

And show it to the world.

Remember the seeds of our desires, sown at Yule

We nurtured them.

They stirred in the ground at Imbolc,

Began to grow at the Equinox,

Now they are sturdy plants,

Strong and bright and growing with the Sun.

As the land becomes green and the plants blossom,

So let our aspirations grow.

May we be as strong in our purpose

As the trees that grow ever upwards.

May we be as courageous

As the flowers that shake in the wind.

May we use all our talents and our creativity

To help the world, other people and ourselves.

So mote it be.

Everyone holds hands in the circle. Someone says:

Now may the Earth be fruitful.

May the trees become green, blossom and bear fruit.

May we be kind to the Earth

And kind to each other.

May our creative thoughts be fruitful

For the good of all.

If anyone has a Tibetan bowl, ring it now while people concentrate for two minutes. If there is no bowl, just concentrate. Then someone says:

Welcome the Goddess and God into our hearts.

Be aware of them within us throughout the year.

For however hard we may seek,

If we do not find the answers within us,

We will never find them without us.

May we accept the gifts of the Goddess and God with pleasure.

May we see in the hardships the lessons that we need to learn.

- Cakes and wine

Blessing

Beltane is:

>The birds and the green and the brightness,
>
>The song and the dance and the ancient play.
>
>Growth and flowering and creativity,
>
>Energy and love and passion.
>
>May the Goddess of flowers, love and beauty
>
>And the God of strength and vitality,
>
>Bless you and keep you all this Beltane night,
>
>And may you remember the spirit of May Day
>
>Through the thirteen moons to come.

All say:

>Blessed be.

Close the circle. Then, if appropriate, jumping the Beltane fire can take place outside.

CHAPTER 6

LITHA

Litha falls between 20 and 23 June, depending on the movements of the Sun. Consult an astrological chart or diary for the precise date.

Litha is the Roman name for the Summer Solstice, but it is probably not as widely used as other old festival names such as Yule or Samhain. Many people simply refer to it as Midsummer or the Summer or Midsummer Solstice. In this book the terms are used interchangeably.

The Summer Solstice is the date of the longest day and shortest night when the Sun is at the height of its powers. Celebration, feasting, bonfires and praise of the God in his representation as the Sun are all part of this festival. It is a joyful time when we compare the abundance in Nature with the abundance of gifts that the Goddess and God offer us in our lives and give thanks for them. Warmth, friendship, passion and love are very evident in these long summer days and it is also a time for forgetting past cares, healing relationships and settling old differences.

The tasks, projects and life changes that we have nurtured and watched over since Yule are growing strongly with the Sun towards maturity. The long days and the warmer weather give us the energy to see them through. Very soon, as with the leaves on the trees, growth will stop. As the Sun grows, pauses and changes course, so we must pause now and take stock of what has happened. In nature, some flowers have already dropped to produce seeds. In the same way, some of our tasks may be complete or no longer relevant. Others may need a final push or ripening before the harvest to achieve their full potential. On some trees and plants, all the leaves are produced before Midsummer and then, when the plant has stopped growing, the flowers bloom. In our lives, this may be the time for the flowering of our achievements.

One thing in particular that we recognise at Midsummer is that achievement brings change either in outlook or circumstance, or both. It is therefore a time when we experience the constantly turning Wheel and accept that nothing stays the same. We journey through the year and we journey through our lives, growing and changing as we go.

Litha is also tinged with sadness. It marks the beginning of the waning year. As the Sun prepares to sink in the sky, so the God must prepare to die.

GODDESS AND GOD

The Goddess is now lover and Mother. Mature and sensuous, she is pregnant with the young God, who will be born at Yule and, as the Earth Mother, she is also pregnant with the harvest. The God is strong and virile and at the height of his powers. Their love is passionate and undying. They rejoice in the warmth and light and in each other but they both know that the God must soon turn away. He has achieved all he can in the Upper Realms of the Earth. Now he must begin his journey to the Land of Shadows.

At Litha, the God is represented by the Sun and by fire, and the Goddess by flowers and a cauldron of water.

A FESTIVAL OF LIGHT AND DARK

Fire and the Sun are the main themes of Litha. The Sun is at its most powerful, the corn in the fields is tall and strong and everything is lush and full. The Earth is abundant, responding to the heat and light of the Sun, and is pregnant with the harvest.

As at Yule, there are several days leading up to this Solstice when you can feel the anticipation in the air. Instead of the calm stillness felt at

Yule, at Litha there is a feeling of steady movement and powerful and strong growth. Everything is reaching outwards and upwards as far as it can before the Wheel turns again and all growth stops as the fruits, seeds and grains ripen for the harvest. On the actual day of the Solstice, everything hovers before growth slowly begins to shut down. For the few days either side of the festival, the Sun appears to rise and set in the same places, as though it is pausing before going away.

We celebrate the light, the growth and the coming harvest with joy but, at the very moment of greatest light, the Sun will begin to pull away from the Earth. In the middle of summer, even though the hottest days may be yet to come, we recognise that winter follows behind.

THE OAK KING AND THE HOLLY KING

The other story of the God at Litha is the opposite of that at Yule. The Oak King, who presides over the waxing year, has come to the end of his reign. He must once again fight the Holly King, Lord of the Waning Year, and this time he loses. Soon after the Solstice, you notice the leaves on the deciduous trees becoming dull and dusty and no more will be produced, but the leaves on the holly continue to shine. It is also said that the wren, the bird symbol of the waning year, will from now on be seen more than the robin.

Although it is unusual for Mummers' plays to be performed around the Summer Solstice, I have included a play here, to match the one for Yule, to give an understanding of the Oak and Holly Kings' part in the Wheel.

LITHA AND FOLK CUSTOMS

BONFIRES

The lighting of bonfires on Midsummer Eve and Midsummer Day is an age-old tradition, practised throughout Europe and also in north-west Africa. The custom is certainly pre-Christian and it continued in certain

places into the nineteenth century. At one time, Midsummer fires and beacons burned all over Britain, even, in the sixteenth century, in the centre of London. By the nineteenth century it was mainly restricted to the so-called Celtic areas of the British Isles – Cornwall, Wales, Ireland, the Isle of Man and the Shetland and Orkney Islands of Scotland. After that, communal bonfires gradually died out.

The fires celebrated and imitated the power of the Sun and, in some places, were a kind of 'sympathetic magic' performed as an attempt to stop the Sun from going away from the Earth or to boost its power as it started to wane. The flames, ashes and smoke were believed to bring protection, good luck and blessings to people, land, crops and livestock.

Some fires were lit from charred logs kept from the previous year and some from embers carried from dwellings. Some were traditionally made from specific types of wood, numbering three or nine, and some were fuelled with animal bones. In the Shetland Islands, broken and unwanted household items were added to the flames and blazing tar barrels lined the streets in Penzance. Out in the country, the fires were lit on hilltops where the Sun could be seen for longer in the sky. In London, lines of bonfires were lit in the streets and were fuelled and tended by the people, while oil lamps burned outside every house and torches were paraded through town. One of the benefits of these street fires was that everyone was out enjoying themselves, enabling old arguments to be settled between neighbours and the rich to spread out tables for the poor.

Wherever they were lit, the Midsummer fires were always at the centre of feasting and merrymaking. Wrestling, running and dancing were all common and the streets of London saw grand torch-lit parades complete with giants and Morris dancers. Various charity collections were made, some for the Church and others to provide ale and bread for the poor. People leapt the flames or danced around or in between the fires. When the fires were out, small pieces of the charred embers were taken away for luck. More details are given in Ronald Hutton's book *Stations of the Sun*.

BLESSING CROPS AND HERDS

The Midsummer fires were a means of blessing and protecting crops and animals. In Herefordshire, the fires were actually lit in the fields and, in the Isle of Man, they were lit so that the prevailing wind would carry the smoke over the crops. In other places, torches lit from the main fire were carried round the fields or placed in vegetable gardens or around cattle sheds and stables. In Somerset a flaming torch was actually passed over and under cattle and horses. In apple-growing counties, there were ceremonies for blessing the trees.

THE FIRE-WHEEL

The wheel, based on four crossing lines or an equal armed cross, has been a frequent symbol of the Sun's passage through the year. The Midsummer custom of setting light to a wheel and rolling it down a hill has been recorded in Britain and France from the fourth to the nineteenth centuries and is probably older. In Glamorgan it was thought to bring good luck if the flames stayed alight all the way down the hill. In Devon, eventually rolling the wheel into a stream was thought to be beneficial for the whole community. A fire-wheel has always been a part of our Midsummer celebration, not as a flaming cart-wheel but as a wheel of flowers.

DIVINATION

Midsummer night has always been regarded as the most efficacious time on which to discover the identity of your future husband and mostly, herbs and plants were used in the divination process. Sowing seeds or strewing petals in a churchyard at midnight and waiting for the image of your lover to appear behind you was one of the most popular ways. Another way was to place a dish of flour under a rosemary bush at sunset. In the morning your future husband's initials would be imprinted in it.

THINGS TO DO

LIGHT AND SHADOW

This is a very simple way of experiencing light and dark, sunshine and shadow. On a warm, sunny day during the two weeks around the Solstice, go out somewhere and find a deciduous tree (one that loses its leaves in winter). It must have plenty of room around it so you can walk round it and sit under it.

Walk clockwise around the tree, staying in the sunlight. See how dense its leaves are. These leaves have been growing and developing since the first buds burst in spring. Now, at Midsummer, there are as many leaves as the tree will grow this year. Some are still young and fresh and bright green, others are older and have turned darker. Look at how the leaves move in the breeze, how the sunlight makes them shine. Then look under the tree at the shade. The more leaves on the tree, the more shade there will be. The leaves grew because of the light of the Sun. It is the light that has produced the shadow.

The Sun, like the tree, is at the height of its growth. Now sit down and experience its warmth and think of all the gifts of the Sun: comfort, light, food, health (vitamin D), vitality, the growth of green leaves, summer flowers and the pleasures of the summer itself. There are many more, so add your own. Give thanks to the Sun. Now go and sit under the tree in the shade. At first, you may shiver and think that the shadows bring no gifts at all, but they do. Without the dark, sleep would be difficult; without the shade of the trees some hot climates would be difficult to bear; having too much sun could cause sunburn or sunstroke. As you sit there, think of other advantages of the shadows. Thank the tree for providing the shade. By understanding first the light and then the shade you will begin to see how the shadow and the light both play equal parts in our lives.

Just after dawn, on the first Midsummer after my initiation, I was surprised by the person who had been my teacher, knocking on the door with presents for all the family. It was a gorgeous sunny morning and he made us go out into the garden to receive them. I had to promise to make a surprise visit myself to someone else the following year, which I did. In turn, I also requested that the family whom I visited repeated the custom. Doing it this way, by passing on the gift-giving just once, prevents the festival from becoming like Yule with presents for everyone. It also maintains the surprise element and it enables you to give a token of appreciation to the person or people who for some reason have meant a lot to you in the past year. Maybe they have helped you through a bad patch, put themselves out to help you or simply been true and loyal friends. On the other hand, they may be people (or a single person) that you want to help or have helped in some way and your gifts will be tokens of your continuing friendship and your wishes for better times ahead. Another reason for choosing someone to receive the gift is to make amends and patch up differences. This may need greater courage, but it is worth it in the end.

To start the custom, first choose the person or people to whom you wish to give presents. Then think about the presents. Don't make them big, they just need to be small tokens and they are even better if you can make them yourself. For example, you could fill small cloth bags with dried herbs, make a pentagram from twigs, make a small embroidery, make sweets, thread some beads, paint a pebble or thread a holed stone onto red cord. Flowers or herbs you have grown yourself are also suitable. There will probably also be more specific appropriate things for the person or people you have chosen to visit. The night before, once you have made and/or wrapped your gift, ask the Goddess and God to bless it. Hold it between your hands and imagine the light of the Midsummer Sun flowing through you and into the gift. Then say:

Lord and Lady of the Sun,

Bless this task I have begun,

That it may be a gift of love,

A gift that will my friendship prove.

Nothing in return I need,

But that it be a growing seed,

That there may be passed from friend to friend

Summer wishes without end.

I ask this blessing with harm to none,

By the power of the rising Midsummer Sun.

Once done, the gift-giving may never come back to you again, but you have started a chain of Midsummer good wishes that could continue year after year.

MAKING A FIRE-WHEEL

There are two ways of making a fire-wheel. If you can obtain enough trailing ivy without destroying a plant, trespassing on other people's property or making a mess, use that. If you can't, buy a wreath or wicker base from a florist or garden centre. The size does not matter, but it needs to be used comfortably in your circle. Very often, you will be able to re-use this base for several years. This type of wreath need not have crosspieces, but a simple circle of flowers will do just as well.

You will also need to buy flowers in various shades of red, yellow and orange.

If you are making an ivy wreath, all you need for the base are long pieces of flexible, trailing ivy. If they are long enough and they are wound correctly, they will hold themselves together, but if you are making a wheel for the first time, you may feel more at ease if you have some florist's wire or green gardener's string handy as a back-up should everything fall apart! Take one length of ivy and bend it round into a circle about 40cm in diameter. Wind any overlap round and round the

other end. Take another piece of ivy and, starting opposite the first overlap, wind it round the first piece, tucking the end in between the two lengths. When you have a circle four stems thick, make the cross pieces. Take three long ivy stems. Put two together and wind the third around it. Push the ends through the side of the wheel from the inside, pull them through, wind them round and tuck them in. Push the other ends in and again tuck them in the outside stems. Take three more stems and do the same thing to make a crosspiece. To keep the centres together, take another stem, tuck it into the top of the wheel by the join of the crosspiece and ring, bring it down to the centre, wrap it round where the arms cross and take it down to the bottom. Do the same with the other arm. Now keep going round the circle with more lengths of ivy, winding them round and tucking in the ends. Try to put a thin end against a thick end so you end up with an even shape. The finished outside needs to be about 4cm thick. Cut flowers with stems of about 7.5cm and tuck them into the twined stems of ivy.

If you are using a florist's wreath, insert the flowers as is best for the style of wreath. If you have a wicker base, insert the flowers as for the ivy wreath.

FIRE-WHEEL RITUAL

The fire-wheel can be your only ritual on the night of the Solstice, or it can be a part of a larger ritual. If this is going to be the case, leave the wheel propped up against the right-hand side (the God side) of the altar as a decoration until you need it and return it there afterwards. Have a cauldron of different coloured flowers on the left side to represent the Goddess.

Place the cauldron of flowers in the centre of the circle. If you have a central fire, stand the cauldron beside it. Say:

This is the cauldron of the Goddess,
Who stays in the centre of the wheel,

Unchanging,

But showing her three aspects,

As Maiden, Mother and Crone.

May the blessings of the Goddess be on us all.

Take up the fire-wheel and hold it up. Say:

This is the Wheel of the Turning Year,

The Wheel of the God

Symbol of the Sun.

Turning through the seasons,

It brings into balance light and dark.

If you are working alone, slowly walk clockwise around your circle carrying the wheel. If you are working with others, stand in a circle together, alternating male and female if possible. Starting from the altar, pass the wheel clockwise around the circle. When saying the rhyme, everyone present says the 'Turn the wheel' lines and a single voice reads the rest. Keep it going and don't break the rhythm.

Turn the wheel, turn the wheel,

Through stations of the Sun,

Turn the wheel, turn the wheel,

The journey's never done.

Turn the wheel, turn the wheel,

The Sun is at his height,

Turn the wheel, turn the wheel,

All the world is light.

Turn the wheel, turn the wheel,

The harvest does begin,

Turn the wheel, turn the wheel,

The harvest's gathered in.

Turn the wheel, turn the wheel,
Warmth and light have fled,
Turn the wheel, turn the wheel,
Remembering the dead.

Turn the wheel, turn the wheel,
Descend into the night,
Turn the wheel, turn the wheel,
Welcome back the light.

Turn the wheel, turn the wheel,
The seeds are in the Earth,
Turn the wheel, turn the wheel,
Waiting for rebirth.

Turn the wheel, turn the wheel,
Welcome King and Queen,
Turn the wheel, turn the wheel,
The leaves are growing green.

Turn the wheel, turn the wheel,
The Sun is at his height,
Turn the wheel, turn the wheel,
All the world is light.

Turn the wheel, turn the wheel,
Through stations of the Sun,
Turn the wheel, turn the wheel,
The journey's never done.

Hold the wheel over the cauldron and say:
    We thank the Goddess and the God for assisting us in our journey

through the Wheel of the Year and the Wheel of our lives. Blessed be.

Return the wheel and the cauldron to the altar.

After Midsummer, leave the wreath outside so that it dies with the dying Sun. The remains of the ivy wreath can be put on the next Sabbat bonfire. The bought wreath can be cleaned off and stored for future use.

THE MIDSUMMER FIRE

Fire, in some form, is an important part of the Midsummer festival. However, it is equally important that, by lighting a fire, you do not destroy even a small patch of the countryside. Never light fires on other people's land unless you have permission. If you have permission to light a fire, don't light it directly on the grass. Make a fire-pit as described for Beltane on page 131. If you are in doubt, use a candle in a lantern.

We always have the fire alight before any ritual begins. It is then made very clear to everyone that the strength of the Sun and the fulfilment of the powers of the God and Goddess are the central part of the ritual.

SPIRAL DANCE

This dance illustrates the continuing spiral of going in towards the dark and coming out again towards the light. You can walk the spiral alone or with a group. When working with a group, everyone holds hands in a circle around the fire. If there aren't enough people to make a circle, hold hands in a line. Two people in the circle, the leader and the back-marker must be very aware of what is going on at all times to prevent the spiral from going too fast and to make sure that people don't let go. To begin, they stand side by side as a part of the circle, the back-marker on the left and the leader on the right. To keep up the impetus, it is best to do this to a drumbeat or to a suitable song or tune. The chant 'Everything flows' given in the ritual on page 166 can also be used. The

traditional tune 'The Horse's Bransle' (pronounced brawl) also fits very well. Before beginning the dance, the leader says:

The Wheel of the Year turns.

At the height of brightness

Is the beginning of the descent into darkness.

In the ending, there is a new beginning.

After the beginning comes change,

Then an end

And another beginning.

Life is a spiral dance of endings and beginnings.

Begin moving in a clockwise circle. Once everyone is moving at the same speed, the leader breaks off from the back-marker and, leading the rest of the circle, begins to walk in a spiral towards the centre, making smaller and smaller circles. When he/she reaches a point close to the fire, he/she changes direction and begins to move in an outgoing spiral. You will now find that alternating lines of people will be going in different directions. Keep going until everyone is in a circle again but facing outwards and then begin again on an in-going spiral. Change direction once more at the centre and spiral outwards until everyone is in a circle again, in the correct places, facing inwards as they started. The leader and back-marker join hands again for a final few steps or a complete circle, whichever you choose.

Circle dances and spirals generate a lot of power so, when you come to a stop, this must be channelled. Everyone first drops down to the ground and puts their hands flat on the floor/earth (depending on where you are). The leader says:

May the power we have raised be used for good in the world, for successful harvests and the harmony of peoples. So mote it be.

Jumping the fire can also be done, as for Beltane (page 130), changing the words to suit Midsummer.

Giving Thanks for Gifts

In the world around us, the gifts of the Goddess and God are at their most evident at Midsummer, and this is also true in our lives, especially when we try to match our lives to the Wheel of the Year. We therefore have a lot to be thankful for. At some time during the week before the Solstice, find time to meditate on the gifts that you have: your personal talents and abilities and your ability to use them; the successful completion or progress of projects and tasks that you set out to achieve at the beginning of the year; your family, friends and relationships; your health; your job. Then look further out and find the good in the world around you. There are quite a number of things that need improvement, but there is also a lot of good. For a start, we live in a peaceful and relatively prosperous country where we are allowed freedom of thought. Think on these things and give thanks to the Goddess and God. By the Midsummer fire, say:

> Lord and Lady of the Summer's light,
> Giving each to the other this magical night,
> Bringing the flowers and ripening grain,
> Giving us talents – no one the same,
> You have brought us fulfilment of dreams
> And filled our cup, until it seems
> That joy and love will overflow,
> So gifts on others we can bestow.
> For granting all that we desire,
> We give you thanks by the Midsummer fire.

Sharing Gifts

Once you have realised just how much you have in this life, think about sharing for the good of others. You can give to a charity that benefits the Earth, people or animals. You can also give your time to helping people, for example taking an older person shopping or giving a carer a break. There are many ways of giving, so match your abilities to the way that you give.

ALTAR AND DECORATIONS

Use gold or deep yellow candles and decorate the altar with white, orange and yellow flowers and green leaves. The cloth should be yellow or orange.

Put vases of summer flowers of a mixture of colours around the house. Add tall grasses with different shaped seed heads, which represent optimum growth and preparation for the harvest.

CAKES AND WINE

Many people make Moon cakes for rituals, using a mixture of ground almonds and honey, and shaping them into small crescent shapes. For Litha, I take the same mixture as for Dark Moon cakes (see page 44) and make it into Sun cakes. Use yellow or orange food colouring instead of black, and form the mixture into about 30 small, flat rounds. Using a knife, imprint an equal-sided cross or eight-pointed star on each one. Bake them as for Dark Moon Cakes.

Some people, especially children, are allergic to food colouring. It is important that you find out if this applies to anyone who is going to be eating the cakes. If so, skip the colouring and simply print the cakes with the cross or star. The same applies to nuts. If anyone has a nut allergy, put a different kind of biscuit on the plate for them.

Golden flowers drink

This combines the gold of the Sun and the flowers of the Goddess and is very easy to make. Simply mix together equal parts of orange juice and elderflower wine and chill for about 30 minutes.

LITHA INCENSE

2 teaspoons frankincense grains

1 teaspoon myrrh grains

1 teaspoon gum benzoin

1 teaspoon crushed dried marigold petals

½ teaspoon crushed dried camomile flowers

2 drops neroli oil

THE OAK KING AND THE HOLLY KING

This is intended to complement the play for Yule, so the characters and many of the words have been kept the same.

Characters

WISE WOMAN

WISE MAN

OAK KING

HOLLY KING

WREN

ROBIN

WISE WOMAN:

Pray silence, my sisters and brothers,

And take heed to our play,

We've come to make a merry rhyme,

All on this Solstice Day.

Listen to us and you shall hear

The story of the Wheel's turn.

So take your ease and listen

While the Midsummer fires do burn.

WISE MAN:

There are two kings that rule the year

Oak waxing and Holly waning,

And twice a year they meet to fight,

Each one the kingdom claiming.

But don't just listen to what I say,

Walk in, King Holly, and clear the way.

HOLLY KING:

In comes I, the Holly King,
From the other side of the year I came.
With my spiked crown and berries red
A king of greatest fame.
I watched over the year's waning,
But since Yule in the ground I've lain.
And now I come this Solstice night,
To fight the Oak King once again.
I saw the Oak King standing by,
He took an oath that I should die.
I'll cut him down all in his prime,
And banish him away until another time.

OAK KING:

In comes I, the Oak King,
In the year's brightest days, of me they sing.
My leaves spreading in rich array,
Give people joy on the longest day.
I reign through the waxing of the year,
And I'll fight King Holly if he be here
His leaves are sharp, his berries unformed,
But my leaves are gentle, I bear acorns.
Holly King, you cannot challenge me,
The sky is yet light, my people agree.

HOLLY KING:

Oak King, your people look forward to the dark,
And winter days when they rest early from work.
The Sun is too strong now, the days are too long,
And soon will come harvest and the wind's autumn song.
My thorns may be hidden beneath your green shade,

But soon they will thicken and my berries grow red
And now, as ruler I must take my turn,
Put up your sword, and this lesson learn.

OAK KING:
I'll put up my sword to defend my throne,
And I'll fight well for the crown before I'm done.

WISE MAN:
See how they fight long and hard for the crown,
But the Oak King has won, King Holly goes down.

WISE WOMAN:
No wonder it looks like the Oak King has won,
For the people need shelter from the burning Sun.
They love Oak's green leaves and the welcoming shade
Of his wide spreading branches in the woodland glade.
But the Wheel it must turn, the year must go round,
So I call on Lady Wren to heal this wound.

WREN:
In comes I, the Wren so small,
I come to heal my master.
I come at his call.

WISE MAN:
How can you heal him, Wren?

WREN:
I will pluck from my breast some feathers brown,
The colour of Earth and the woodland ground.

I'll lay them on his wound so deep,

Their magic will bring him round from his sleep

ALL SING:

Now the Oak tree bears an acorn

As earth it is brown,

And the King of the Holly he will rise from the ground,

And the King of the Holly our ruler he will be,

But the first tree of the summer, it is the Oak tree,

Oak tree, Oak tree,

And the first tree of the Summer, it is the Oak Tree.

WISE MAN:

And so King Holly rises, tall and strong,

And once again, the battle is long.

But now, the Oak King he goes down.

King Holly has won the waning year's crown.

WISE WOMAN:

But the people still need the strength of the Sun

To ripen their grain before summer is done.

There's many a day before leaves will be shed,

So I call on Lord Robin with breast so red.

ROBIN:

In comes I, Robin of the Wood

Servant of the Oak King, who has shed his blood.

WISE MAN:

Can you heal this King?

ROBIN:

I can heal him, so he will stay

To watch over the first harvest on Lammas Day,

But his growth it will cease and his leaves they will die

For Holly is King, we cannot deny.

WISE MAN:

How will you heal him?

ROBIN:

The Oak King has a lady, the rose in her bower,

The sweetest of all the summer flowers.

Her thorn is sharp, but her heart is sweet

She blooms throughout the summer's heat.

When the Lady Rose lies down by his side,

The Oak will rise and take her for his bride.

WISE WOMAN:

Together they will grace the long summer days,

But, come the harvest, they will start to fade.

WISE MAN:

Then the days will become short again.

And the Holly King truly begins his reign.

'Twixt Mabon and Samhain, when autumn winds howl,

The Oak King's leaves will drop to the ground.

WISE WOMAN:

But soon once more the Wheel will turn,

And the old story again we'll learn.

ALL SING:

Now the Oak tree bears green leaves
As thick as the grass,
But the Sun will grow weaker as the summer days pass.
And the Sun will grow weaker the winter to foresee,
And the first tree of the summer it was the Oak tree.
Oak tree, Oak tree,
And the first tree of the summer, it was the Oak tree.

WISE WOMAN:

And now our story we have told,
A tale of wisdom for young and old.
From the parts we played let us be set free,
And our own true selves we now shall be.

A COMPLETE MIDSUMMER RITUAL

Draw the circle and invoke the Goddess and God as on page 18. Share out the words as you think fit or let one person say them. Those parts that everyone says together should be written and given out, or gone over at the beginning of the appropriate section. Have a fire, or candle in a lantern, burning in the centre of the circle and a fire wheel and a cauldron of flowers by the altar. A male voice begins by saying:

The Oak King, the Sun King,
Shows his full glory,
The height of his powers
On this Midsummer Night.
He comes to the Goddess,
The Queen of the Summer.
True love is theirs,
Fulfilled and complete.

Everyone replies:

    Everything flows,

    Nothing is still,

    Life is a journey

    Through time and space.

A female voice says:

    The Earth Mother dances

    With joy for her lover,

    Lays down beside him,

    Is filled with his warmth.

    Goddess and God,

    This day united,

    Bringing together

    Her water, his fire.

Everyone replies:

    Everything flows,

    Nothing is still,

    Life is a journey

    Through time and space.

A male voice says:

    A change of direction

    Is born of completion.

    The King at his strongest

    Must now turn away.

    He must set out

    On the road to the Dark Lands,

    Safe in the love

    Of the Goddess, his Queen.

Everyone replies:

> Everything flows,
> Nothing is still,
> Life is a journey
> Through time and space.

A female voice says:

> The Goddess alone
> Is something unchanging,
> Showing three aspects,
> Never to fade.
> Foreseeing the death,
> Of Her Son and her Lover,
> Her arms she wraps round him,
> Accepting the fate.

Everyone replies:

> Everything flows,
> Nothing is still,
> Life is a journey
> Through time and space.
> Everything flows,
> Nothing is still.
> Life is a journey
> Through time and space.

Then use the ideas suggested earlier in this chapter to cover all the following activities:

- The play of the Holly King and the Oak King
- The Fire-wheel ritual
- Spiral dance

- Giving thanks for gifts (if this is the first time the idea has been given to people, read out the introductory paragraph as well as the rhyme).

A male voice says:

> Sun King, we call upon your power.
>
> Shine on your Goddess
>
> And shine on the Earth.
>
> May your warmth be ever with us
>
> Even as you turn towards the dark.
>
> May it ripen the fruits
>
> And make good the harvest.
>
> Blessed be.

A female voice says:

> Goddess, in your three aspects,
>
> Help us to achieve our goals.
>
> Help us to recognise and be glad in the achievements.
>
> Help us to accept the change that they bring,
>
> As you accept the death of your Lover,
>
> For all these changes are for the good of the Earth.
>
> Blessed be.

- Cakes and wine

Blessing

The Solstice is:

> Sweet rain and green grass,
>
> Hot sun and growing crops,
>
> Birdsong and flowers,
>
> Fertility and growth,
>
> The scent of herbs and the taste of strawberries,
>
> The swelling of fruits and the spreading of leaves,
>
> Warmth and strength, passion and love,

The fulfilment of wishes and the beginnings of dreams.

May your dreams come true this Solstice Night.

Blessed be.

Close the circle.

CHAPTER 7

LAMMAS

Lammas is celebrated either on 1 August or on the evening of 31 July. This festival has two main names, Lughnasadh (with various spellings, usually to do with knocking off the 'd' or 'h' or both), and Lammas. Lughnasadh is the Celtic name and means the mourning or remembrance of Lugh, the Sun God, for on this day he lays down his life for the sake of the harvest. Lammas is of Saxon origin, coming from the words *hlaef mas*, or loaf mass, the celebration of the bread. Since Saxon times, it has been used in both the farming and the Christian Church calendar. Use whichever you feel the most comfortable with. Other names are First Harvest, First Fruits and, if you celebrate on 31 July, August Eve.

THE FESTIVAL AND ITS MEANING

The two names for the festival point to the fact that it is both a time to celebrate and a time to remember the passing of the God and the year. At Lammas we celebrate the first harvest. Fruits and berries are ripening, seeds are being scattered and the first of the corn is being cut. But the days are noticeably shorter; the colours of the countryside are the browns of dry grasses, dotted with mourning purples, whites and blood-scarlet poppies. Although the weather may still be hot and the time of year means 'holidays' for many people, the Sun is dropping and the year is beginning to die.

Lammas is another outdoor festival and, because of the time of year, I often find myself on holiday at Lammas time, so I have celebrated by the seashore, on a campsite and even outside some holiday chalets. When this happens, I always take my bundle of barley or wheat away with me so that I can make my Mary Barleycorn (see below) and hang her up in the tent. Wherever you may be living or staying, try to get outside to see the changes that are taking place. In countryside hedgerows, tall, dry grasses are dropping their seeds, combines are at work in the fields and maybe the first blackberries will be ready for picking. In town parks annual flowers may still be a riot of colour, but seeds are flying from sycamore and lime trees, and rowan berries are turning red.

At Lammas, we look at how the tasks that we set ourselves at the beginning of the year are faring. Some of them will be complete and these make up our first harvest. We acknowledge that, for the sake of this harvest, and also for the sake of the harvest of grain all over the world, the God has made himself a willing sacrifice and the Goddess has willingly let him go.

It is therefore a time to think of how great a role the Goddess and God play in our lives, and to give thanks for it. We make a Mary Barleycorn as symbol of the Goddess, hold her up in our ritual and hang her in the house. We count our blessings and pledge to share our gifts and we acknowledge the God's sacrifice by promising to make a sacrifice for someone in need. Like the wild grasses, we scatter seeds, hoping that they will do some good in the world and, at the end of it all, we play silly games and have a celebration.

There is still, however, more hard work to be done before Mabon, the next festival, by which time all the harvest should be gathered in.

GODDESS AND GOD

For the last time, God and Goddess lie together in the heat of the dying Sun. Around them, the corn grows golden like the hair of the God, scattered with poppies, red as his blood. The Goddess, as the Earth Mother, brown and beautiful, with the last flowers of summer entwined in her hair, is heavily pregnant with the harvest. They have grown and loved together through the long summer days, but now it is time for the God to sacrifice himself so that his power will go into the Earth and into the food that it provides. He will be taken into the Earth and will re-emerge on the other side as the God of Death and Resurrection and Lord of the Shadowlands. The Goddess will now gradually become the wise Crone of Winter. We celebrate and give thanks for the gifts that they provide but mourn with the Goddess the loss of her partner.

LAMMAS AND FOLK CUSTOMS

HARVEST BEGINS

Before reaping machines and combine harvesters, corn was cut by hand with a sickle. Harvest was highly labour-intensive, so everyone in the village was employed at this time of the year and often itinerant groups of workers formed 'harvest gangs', travelling from farm to farm. The reapers went through the field first, cutting down the corn. Behind them came the binders to tie it into sheaves which were leant upright, a few together, into stooks. After a few days drying in the sun, the stooks would be tossed onto a cart and taken back to the barn, where they were stacked, ready for threshing. Harvest usually lasted through the whole of August and so was very dependent on the weather. Even if the first few days were sunny, no one could guarantee the whole of the crop being taken in without disasters. You had to move quickly when the time was right.

Organisation of the harvest workers was in the charge of a trusted employee, sometimes chosen by the farmer and sometimes elected by his fellow workers. In some counties, he was known as the Lord (or Mylord) and his second-in-command was known as the Lady. Whether these names were a throwback to earlier times, when the Lord and Lady of the harvest were recognised as the Goddess and God, is not known. The names had very early on become a part of country terminology.

The Lord was responsible for drawing up a contract with the farmer, stating that his harvest would be brought in by a certain date. The farmer, for his part, had to provide a small feast to mark the start of the harvest, a set daily amount of beer or cider for the workers and the food and drink for the 'harvest home' celebrations when all the corn was safely in store.

Different harvest customs existed all over the country. In East Anglia, a harvest horn was blown around the village at the start of each day to ensure workers would get to the fields on time. In other places it was blown to mark mealtimes. Initiation ceremonies for youngsters working on their first harvest often ended in their promising to buy beer for the rest of the company out of their first harvest money. One of the things done to them was to have a nail driven into the bottom of their shoe until they shouted 'Beer!'. All harvest workers were also allowed to ask for 'largesse' (a gift of money for the feast) from passing travellers. This happened in a number of ways, including standing round the unsuspecting person and chanting or shouting until the gift was handed over. A successful encounter was finished by more shouts from the Lord and three cheers with raised sickles from the rest of the company. The custom was known as 'hollering largesse'.

For the Saxon *hlaef mas*, the first sheaves of wheat to be cut were quickly dried and threshed, and the wheat ground into flour. Loaves or flat bannocks were baked and used as a ceremonial offering by way of

thanks for the harvest to come. The custom was taken over into Christian custom and bread from the first sheaves was blessed in church after which it was either distributed to the poor, crumbled back into the fields or crumbled into the four corners of the barn as protection for the gathered harvest. In more recent years, organic farmers and independent millers and bakers organised a Lammas loaf race, to see who would be first to cut and grind the corn and bake it into bread.

GAMES, FAIRS AND REVELS

Going back further than Medieval or Saxon times, the Celtic inhabitants of the British Isles celebrated their Lughnasadh with games in honour of Lugh, God of the Sun and also of artists, craftsmen and warriors. The games lasted longer than just one day and may have gone on for four weeks, either side of a full Moon. Athletics, trials of strength and horse racing were all included, and the games cemented communities, ensuring peace for the coming year.

THINGS TO DO

LAMMAS MEDITATION

Before considering your harvest and cutting your first ears of wheat, read through the following meditation and remember the main parts of it. Your own mind and imagination will probably fill in details that are special or relevant to you. Then sit in a quiet place where you will not be disturbed and ask the Goddess and God and the Spirits of the Elements to protect you. Take three deep breaths and begin.

You are walking up a lane, overhung by trees in full leaf and edged with tall, dry grasses and purple and white flowers. Beyond a hedge you see a field of wheat. This is your harvest field. You are going to look at the wheat to see if it is ready for cutting. You walk into the field. The corn is tall and rustling in the wind. The Sun is mellow and warm and the air is still. A blackbird gives an alarm call. A wren hops along a branch and cocks his head. Stand quiet, look and listen. You see that some of your wheat is ready for harvest. In your hand you have a sickle. You raise it to cut the wheat, but stop for, in the centre of the field you see two lovers. She is heavily pregnant, golden and blooming, with a garland of cornflowers and poppies in her corn-coloured hair. He is tall and strong, his limbs bronzed, his hair golden, but with a look of sadness in his eyes. The Lord and Lady of the Corn embrace and kiss, look into each other's eyes and solemnly nod. A thrown sickle suddenly flies through the air and strikes the Corn Lord. His blood spurts to the ground and he falls at the Lady's feet. As the God sinks into the Earth, the Mother Goddess spreads her arms in blessing. Then alone, she walks through the field, stopping all growth, but causing grain and fruits to ripen. The harvest can begin. You gather your first sheaf of grain into one hand and cut it with your sickle. You hold it up, it glows in the late summer Sun, and you say: 'I thank the Lord and Lady of the corn for this, my first harvest. May their blessings be upon it and may I use it wisely for the good of all. So mote it be.'

Carrying your harvest, return to the lane. Walk back along it and, in your mind gradually walk back into the place where you are sitting. Begin to be aware of where you are. Thank the Goddess and God and the Spirits of the Elements for being with you. When you are ready, open your eyes and come back. Write your experiences in your Book of Shadows.

ASSESSING YOUR HARVEST

This activity should be done on Lammas day or just before and really gets you thinking carefully about the seeds of projects and tasks that you sowed just after Yule and how they have progressed through the summer. Before you do anything, complete the Lammas Meditation, above. This helps you to realise that it is the Goddess and God who have helped you to bring about your harvest.

In your Book of Shadows, draw as many ears of wheat as seeds that were sowed. How have they fared? Are they ripe? Are they full? Have they turned out as you wanted or imagined? Have some just not grown at all? Were any of them the wrong variety (the wrong sort of project) after all? Remember that each ear contains many grains, the many different aspects of each project or task. Draw them in. Have they all developed equally? Have some been pushed out at the expense of others? Have some been blighted? Consider the ears together. Are some ready for harvest? Will others do better for a little more sunshine and rain? There is still time before Mabon, so only harvest the ears that are ready. Lammas is, after all, the harvest of 'first fruits' and so only the beginning.

Choose an ear of corn that is ripe and ready for harvesting. Draw a line through the stem to represent the sickle cut. Then draw the cut ear of wheat on a separate page. Surround it with a garland of flowers in token of your celebration. Your first fruits should be an offering to the Goddess and God, that you may use them wisely for their sake, so underneath write: 'Through the love of the Goddess and the sacrifice of the God, this harvest has come to be. I give thanks for these gifts and promise to use them wisely for the good of all. So mote it be.'

Between now and Mabon, meditate on the remaining ears of wheat. Nurture them if need be and cut them when they are ready. You may find that you have to do quite a lot of work to make sure that everything you wish to harvest will be ready on time. Between now and Mabon, make the final push. As each of your ears of corn is cut, give thanks for it and draw it on the next page so you end up with a bunch of wheat ears that will make up your last sheaf, or harvest home, that will be celebrated at Mabon.

I AM BOUND TO LEAVE YOU

The tune is the traditional folk tune, 'Are You Going to Leave Me, Love?' It is best sung or spoken, turn and turn about with two voices, the first female, the second male. However, if you are celebrating alone, sing or read it out loud to yourself. Writing it made me appreciate just how much we should be grateful for the harvest that we gather.

Are you going to leave me, love?
Are you going to leave me?
O, would you leave your own love true,
To go to a land that you never knew?

I am bound to leave you, love,
I am bound to leave you.
O, I must leave my own love true,
And go to a land that I never knew.

At Yule you were a babe in my arms
When winter days were cold and dark.
You were the promise of Sun's new light
In berries red and candle bright.

At Imbolc you were welcomed in
Triple Goddess of the spring,
But we were the children wild and free
Delighting in our company.

When the sap rose in the trees,
You came to court me with the Sun.
You danced with longing in your eyes,
We knew that love would be the prize.

On that magic Beltane Eve,
Through brakes and briars you made me run.
I found you there amongst the trees,
There to taste love's ecstasy.

In the heat of the Midsummer Sun
We lay among the growing grain.
But soon the sun it turned away,
And though we loved, you could not stay.

Now, my love, the corn grows high,
The poppies bloom like blood so red.
Your loving eyes do me entice,
But I must be the sacrifice.

Journey safe, my love, my life,
Lord of the Shadows you will be.
And when the harvest is gathered in
I'll come to you and be your Queen.

JOHN BARLEYCORN AND MARY BARLEYCORN

John Barleycorn isn't so much a custom as a song, and a very ancient song at that. It has been said that for every version of an English folk song, it has been one hundred years in existence. There are at least ten versions of the 'John Barleycorn' song, which suggests that the story is about a thousand years old. Three farmers take John Barleycorn to a field, plough and sow and 'harrow him in' and 'swear a solemn oath, John Barleycorn is dead'. But he soon surprises everyone and begins to grow till he is cut down, ground and put into the mashing tub to 'burn his tail'. Then 'when he came out he'd changed his name, for they called him home brewed ale'. It is the old story of the God, sacrificed and transformed for our enjoyment and triumphing over all, 'for Little Sir John in the nut brown bowl proved the strongest man at last'. Making us drunk and laying us flat, he finally gets the better of us.

If John Barleycorn, the 'hero bold' of folk song, is the sacrificed God, Mary Barleycorn represents the Goddess. The concept is not mine but that of an old friend who once wrote a song about her. Mary Barleycorn is the Goddess of the Corn who has willingly given her lover in sacrifice. She knows that, as the dark days come, she will meet him in the Land of Shadows, but for now she is left to give birth to the harvest alone. Use a bundle of barley or wheat to make her, so that you can use her in your ritual and hang her up in your house to remind you that nothing is ever achieved without the blessing of the Goddess and God. At Mabon, decorate her with ribbons in celebration of a completed harvest.

MARY BARLEYCORN

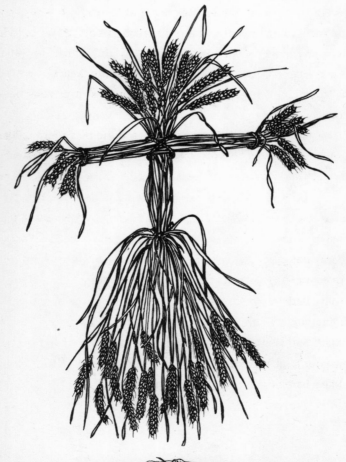

You will need fine cotton string and a bundle of barley, 45–50cm long and about 3.5cm in diameter if held tightly together. Buy this from a shop or garden centre that sells dried flowers. If barley is not available, use wheat or a mixture of wheat and oats. Do not go out into the countryside and cut from a field of barley. That amounts to stealing.

Trim the bottoms of the stalks to make them all the same length. Set aside ten ears of barley for the arms. With the string, make a firm tie around the remaining stalks, 15–18cm from the bottom. Working round the outside of the bunch, fold the stalks downward over the ties to make the 'skirt', leaving 18 in the centre. Tie round at the base of the 18 remaining corn ears to make the 'head'. For the 'arms', divide the ten reserved stalks into bunches of five and lay them together end to end. Tie them together at the base of the corn ears at either end to make 'hands' and to keep the stalks together. Lay the 'arm piece' at right angles across the 'body' of the doll, just under the 'head' and over the original tie. Tie it securely in place. Tie a loop of string at the back for hanging.

Making your Mary Barleycorn can stand alone as a ritual. Make her within your circle and, as you work, remember the sacrifice that both God and Goddess have made for the sake of the harvest. When she is done, hold her up and take her round the circle. Pass her through the incense smoke, over the candle, sprinkle her with water and touch her to your stone. In the centre of the circle, stop and say:

O, Mary Barleycorn,

Goddess of the Earth,

O, Mary Barleycorn,

Bringing all to birth.

O, Mary Barleycorn,

Now your lover's dead.

O, Mary Barleycorn,

The Earth it is his bed.

O, Mary Barleycorn,

You walk the fields alone.

O, Mary Barleycorn,

Blessing all that's grown.

O, Mary Barleycorn,

Ripen fruit and grain.

O, Mary Barleycorn,

Make harvest come again.

O, Mary Barleycorn,

We honour you with love.

O, Mary Barleycorn,

Send blessings from above.

O, Mary Barleycorn,

Bringing all to birth.

O, Mary Barleycorn,

Goddess of the Earth.

BREAD

The loaf that we eat is the symbol of our acceptance of the harvest to use for our own good. Use it also as an offering to the Goddess and God and to the Spirits of the Elements, by way of thanks for their watching over our own inner harvest. It is also a way to remember that not everyone in the world has enough food.

For this short ritual you will need one loaf and four small rolls. The ritual works well when performed outdoors, as you can crumble the bread directly onto the earth and the crumbs can be readily picked up by birds. If you prefer to be indoors, lay the rolls at the four quarters and, at the end of the ritual, put them into a bag to be crumbled outdoors when it is more convenient.

Put the loaf onto a wooden board or a tray, together with a bread knife (or your athame if it is sharp enough). Cast the circle as on page 17. Hold up the bread in the centre of the circle and say:

O Goddess of the Earth,

Who gives birth to the harvest,

All year you have watched over me/us.

All year you have helped my/our seeds to grow.

You sent your love to water them,

As you send the rain to the harvest field.

You have sent your love to warm them,

As you send the sun to the grains of corn,

To draw young shoots to the light,

So that they might bear fruit for the good of all

Now that you prepare to feed the people of the world,

I/we offer you this bread

As a token of thanksgiving that comes from my/our heart(s).

O Lord of the Harvest,

Who has committed to lay down his life for the corn,

All year you have been beside me/us.

You have given your strength,

For my/our seeds to grow strong.

You have given your passion

To help them when they faltered.

You have given your laughter,

For when growth was hard.

Now you lay down your life in the Harvest field,

So that my/our seeds may bear fruit

And the people of the world may be fed.

You have died for the sake of the coming harvest.

I/we pledge to use it well,

And offer you this bread

As a token of thanksgiving that comes from my/our hearts.

Cut the bread into small pieces, hold it up again and say:

I/we give this food to the creatures of the wild,

That they may be fed and grow strong for the winter.

I/we send out my/our wishes that all the peoples of the earth,

Whatever their race or colour or creed,

May be freed from starvation and poverty,

And that those of us who have more than enough,

Will remember to share what we have.

If you wish, at this point, you can pledge to support a chosen charity that works overseas, or one that works with homeless and destitute people in your own country. Leave the bread on the board or tray and, after you have closed the circle, scatter it around in a secluded place where animals and birds can go without being disturbed. Take one of the rolls, go the East quarter and say:

O Guardian Spirits of the East,

I/we thank you for your soft breezes

That have nurtured my/our growing seeds

And positive thoughts that have made them strong.

I/we offer this bread in thanks.

If you are outside, crumble the bread onto the Earth. If you are indoors, lay it down at the East point. Do the same at the South, West and North, saying, in turn:

O Guardian Spirits of the South,

I/we thank you for the warmth of the Sun

That has helped my/our seeds to grow,

And for the fire in my/our heart(s)

That has brought them to the harvest.

I/we offer this bread in thanks.

O Guardian Spirits of the West,
I/we thank you for the rain,
That has swelled my/our seeds,
And the love in my/our heart(s)
That cared for roots and green shoots.
I/we offer this bread in thanks.

O Guardian Spirits of the North,
I/we thank you for the Earth,
Which provided a safe bed for my/our seeds.
And for our my/our different skills
Which helped them to grow.
I/we offer this bread in thanks.

If you wish, sit and meditate on how the aspects of the four Elements have made your particular seeds and projects bear fruit. Then close the circle.

SACRIFICE

We think about sacrifice at Lammas, because the God makes himself a willing sacrifice so that the harvest of the fields and our own harvest can come about. The fact that we have achieved success in our projects and tasks, that we have been seeing as growing and fruiting seeds, means that we will change. A part of our old selves has to be sacrificed so that our new self may flourish. Very often, once we have learned lessons or achieved something, our old self can be shed easily, but sometimes it is hard to let go and it seems to be more of a sacrifice. Think of old habits, old ways and of pastimes and even jobs that may have to be changed.

Have with you your notebook and something to write with. Cast your circle, then say:

O Lady of the Harvest and the ripening grain,

Who willingly accepts that your love must be the sacrifice,

I call upon you.

Show to me the aspects of myself

That I must sacrifice

In order to be reborn.

O Lord of the Harvest and the ripening grain,

You who lay down your life for the corn,

To be reborn as the Lord of the Shadows

I call upon you.

Teach me to make a willing sacrifice,

That I may be reborn.

In your book, write down the things that you have achieved or hope to achieve with this year's harvest. Opposite these things, write what aspect of yourself that needs to be sacrificed, in order that you can take every opportunity that your harvest offers. Take time thinking about this to make sure you get it right. When you have done, stand up and say:

Lord and Lady of the harvest field,

My whole self to you I yield,

My old self I lay down with the corn,

So that my new self may be reborn.

Take a few minutes now, to think how you can make a willing sacrifice for someone else, a relative or friend, or maybe someone disadvantaged that you do not yet know, such as a lonely person in an old people's home or someone in hospital who needs a visit. You can give to a charity, walk a dog, do voluntary work on a nature reserve or anything else that comes into your mind. A sacrifice in these terms is willingly doing a good turn for someone, for which you personally have to give

up something, either materially or in terms of time. When you have thought, voice your sacrifice out loud and write it in your book. Then say:

I make this my sacrifice,

And for it I will ask no price.

For Goddess and God I pledge this deed,

That it may help someone in need.

LAMMAS GAMES

Devise some silly games or find old-fashioned games to play either as part of the celebrations after the main ritual or for a games party in any evening around the main date. Make them outdoor if possible. Three-legged races, quoits and welly-throwing are all good examples of what you can do. If you are on the seashore try throwing pebbles into a hole or seaweed throwing. With a bit of imagination, you can think up enough daft things to fill an evening.

LAMMAS INCENSE

2 teaspoons frankincense

1 teaspoon crumbled cinnamon stick

1 teaspoon crumbled dried orange peel

1 teaspoon dried crumbled yarrow leaves

4 drops sweet orange oil

ALTAR AND DECORATIONS

Have an orange cloth and candles. Decorate the altar with ears of corn and hang bunches of corn around the house. Bowls of seasonal fruits are also appropriate. In vases, mix fresh cornflowers with ears of wheat or oats and artificial poppies (fresh ones drop too quickly).

Poppy seed cake

8oz/225g butter, softened, plus extra for greasing

8oz/225g honey

8oz/225g wholemeal flour

2 tsp baking powder

3 tbsp poppy seeds

4 eggs, beaten

Heat the oven to 350°F/180°C/Gas 4. Butter a shallow baking tin, about 20 x 30cm. Cream the butter in a bowl and beat in the honey. Mix together the flour, baking powder and poppy seeds. Beat the flour mixture and the eggs alternately into the butter and honey. Put the mixture into the buttered tin and smooth the top. Bake the cake for 20 minutes or until it is firm and a skewer stuck into the centre comes out clean. Turn it onto a wire rack to cool and cut it into small squares for serving. (If the cake has only to go round a few people you can halve all the ingredients and use a 20 x 15cm tin.)

Blackberry ale

This is based on barley wine, a strong, sweet beer. If you are working in a group and someone new is joining you for the celebration, you could continue the old harvest custom by asking them to provide the barley wine.

1pint/575ml barley wine

8oz/225g blackberries

2oz/50g demerara sugar

Put the blackberries and sugar into a small saucepan with 2 tbsp water. Cover them and set them on a low heat until the blackberries are soft and juicy. Rub the blackberries and juice through a sieve. Cool the

resulting puree and put it into a jug. Gradually stir in the barley wine. Serve at room temperature. If you are holding your celebrations outside, cover the top of your chalice or tankard with clingfilm to keep out fruit flies!

THE COMPLETE LAMMAS RITUAL

Draw the circle and invoke the Goddess and God as on page 18. The first person says:

> The time of the first harvest is come
> The corn is high,
> The grain is ripe,
> The wind plays over golden fields,
> The sickle is raised in readiness.

The second voice says:

> The time of our harvest is come,
> Our hopes are high,
> Our projects are ripe,
> We have grown and matured in the summer Sun.
> The sickle is raised in readiness.

The third voice says:

> Wait. Before the taking, we must honour and give thanks to those who gave the gifts of the harvest, who made sacrifices of love and life for our sake. Close your eyes and come with me on an inner journey.

Then use the ideas suggested earlier in this chapter to cover all the following activities:

- The Lammas meditation from the beginning to '...sadness in his eyes'
- Song: 'I am bound to leave you' (leaving out last verse)

- The meditation then continues to '…blessing and giving'
- Song: last verse
- Mary Barleycorn
- Bread
- Sacrifice – if you are working alone, do this as described above; if in a group, leave out the writing but allow participants a few minutes to focus on their own thoughts. Begin by saying:

> The God has sacrificed himself for the sake of the harvest.
> The Goddess accepts that he has to go.
> Our successful harvest will bring about changes,
> And parts of ourselves will have to be sacrificed,
> So that a new self can be reborn
> To take our lives forward.

Read out the calls to the Goddess and God, changing 'I' to 'we' where necessary. Then say:

> Let us think about the things that we have achieved or hope to achieve, with this year's harvest. Now we must recognise what needs to be sacrificed, in order that we can take every opportunity that our harvest offers. Think of old habits, old ways and of pastimes and even jobs that may have to be changed.

Another voice can read this, if wished:

> Lord and Lady of the harvest field,
> Our whole selves to you we yield,
> Our old selves we lay down with the corn,
> So that our new selves may be reborn.

The first voice reads instructions about making a sacrifice. Then a second voice says:

We make this our sacrifice,

And for it we will ask no price.

For Goddess and God we pledge our deed,

That it may help someone in need.

So mote it be.

- Cakes and wine

Blessing

We have celebrated the first fruits of our harvest and given thanks for the sacrifice made by Goddess and God for our sake. This is only the beginning. There is still hard work to be done before all the harvest is gathered. May the Goddess and God bless our labours.

Lammas is:

Corn and poppies and dewy mornings,

Scattering seeds and ripening fruit

It is:

Joy and sadness,

Celebration and mourning,

Sacrifice and birth,

Death and rebirth,

Harvesting and scattering,

Waiting and changing.

Hard labour and achievement,

The beginning of the end of the summer.

May your harvest be fruitful

And your work rewarded.

Blessed be.

Close the circle, then enjoy the Lammas games.

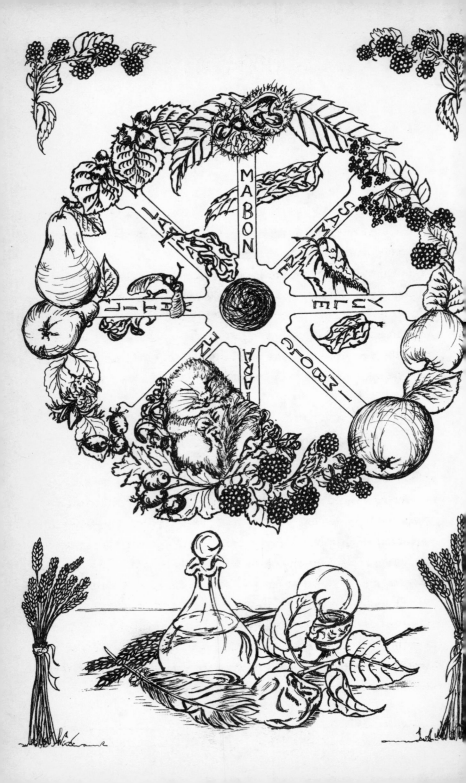

CHAPTER 8

MABON

Mabon can fall at any time between 20 and 23 September, depending on the exact timing of the Equinox. Consult an astrological diary for the precise date.

The festival was apparently given the name of Mabon by Alex Sanders (who originated the branch of Wicca called 'Alexandrian Wicca') in the 1960s. Before then it had simply been known as the Autumn Equinox. Mabon is Welsh for 'son' or 'great son'. Using it to name the Equinox serves as a reminder that the God, like the year, is standing on the threshold of the Underworld.

THE FESTIVAL AND ITS MEANING

Mabon celebrates 'harvest home', the end of the grain harvest. The fields are all cleared, and in the garden most of the crops have come to an end. Only the apples and pears and the winter-hardy plants remain. As the Sun retreats, the Earth pulls in. All growth stops, sap is withdrawn into tree roots and the leaves begin to turn.

It is a time to look over what we have achieved and what we have learned, to give thanks for it all and to share some of our riches. It is a 'winding down' time, for finishing things off and tying loose ends and preparing for the dark days of winter. It is also a time to reflect on the balance of opposite forces in our life, to stop, rest and maybe change gear in time for the meditations of Samhain.

In our own personal harvest, we think of our successes and achievements over the past year, however small. We also take note of the lessons learned from projects that were not so successful. These achievements and lessons are the seeds from which new projects will grow in the future. We celebrate both as gifts of the Goddess and God of the harvest and, at the same time, we clear away the unwanted 'chaff' that no longer has any relevance in our lives.

Mabon is usually celebrated indoors and most of the ritual concentrates on different aspects of our harvest, giving thanks, sharing and healing.

GODDESS AND GOD

At Mabon, the Goddess is the Lady of the fruitful harvest. She has given nearly all she has to give and watches over us while we reap the final sheaves. She is growing old and wise with the year and offers us wisdom, healing and rest. In the Land of Shadows, she receives the dying God with outstretched arms and yet, in her maiden aspect, she is pregnant with the God who will be born at Yule.

The God, having laid down his life for the harvest, is about to cross over into the Land of Shadows. He stands on the threshold of light and dark, life and death. Soon he will rest in the arms of the Goddess, waiting to be reborn. Like the corn, the God has been cut down, but his seed brings the promise of new life.

A TIME OF BALANCE

The theme of balance runs through this festival, the balance of light and dark, life and death, summer and winter, of reviewing the past and looking to the future and of celebrating gifts and clearing away the unwanted. The harvest of the grain symbolises the balance between life and death. The corn has been cut down, the stalks are dead, but the grains will grow again, producing next year's harvest.

Thanksgiving and sharing

Giving thanks for gifts, successes, achievements and gained wisdom should feature highly in the Mabon celebrations and rituals. The Goddess has given us food for our bodies and food for our minds and souls, and the God has given his life that this may happen. We should celebrate and delight in everything that we have received and learned and give thanks to the God and Goddess and to the Spirits of the Elements.

Gifts are best used if they are shared, so we look to see how we can benefit others through the wisdom gained through our achievements. You don't have to go out and actively teach. Even a slight shift of attitude could have made you a more understanding person, for example, or one who is more ready to listen than before. Use your understanding or your new listening ability to help someone who needs advice or just a sympathetic ear. However, simply be ready for these occasions, rather than actively going out and forcing them onto people. If you are ready, a situation will come.

Clearing away and finishing off

Although the corn is gathered, there are still apples, pears and berries left to be picked. This is the time of year to tie up loose ends and also to throw away aspects of your life that are no longer relevant.

If any goal that you set yourself at the beginning of the year remains unfinished, accept that now you have probably come as far as you need to in this particular growth cycle. If you have gone a long way towards achieving it, be pleased with yourself. It was obviously a worthwhile goal and you have done well. Take note of why you didn't quite do what you set out to and make this the 'seed' of next year's achievements. Even if you are half-way there, bring things to a conclusion now and continue, if you wish, in the spring. If one of your 'seeds' or projects has come to nothing, then either it wasn't the right one for you or you may have been attempting something at the wrong time. Mentally throw it out now, without feeling guilty. You may wish to come back to it in the spring or you may realise that it no longer bears any relevance to your life.

Mabon is also a good time of the year to resolve personal relationships. Do you owe someone an apology or have you borrowed something that you ought to give back? Do you need to repair a relationship that has gone sour, or should you simply decide that for the good of both parties you should put it behind you? Only you can decide, but do it now.

A TIME FOR REST AND CHANGE

At the point of the Equinox, there are 24 hours when the world seems to stand still and balance before the Wheel begins to turn again. Ever since the spring, we have been attempting to travel and grow spiritually and have been working towards our goals. Through the first part of September, there is a gentle winding-down and now, at Mabon, everything pauses before the descent into winter. Stand outside and you can feel the Earth drawing in. The Sun is lower; even the sound of the wind in the trees is different. The quality of the light has changed and the fields are all stubble or freshly ploughed. The Earth pulls her fertility from the land. 'Rest,' she says, 'rest and sleep.'

We must prepare for winter now and for a new cycle to begin by putting our house in order. The achievements we have made and the lessons we have learned have inevitably changed us. After Samhain there will be a time to rest while these changes take effect and while we wait until new seeds of ideas come to us.

MABON AND FOLK CUSTOMS

HARVEST HOME

There are no folk customs associated with the actual Equinox, but there are many connected with the end of the grain harvest. In the days before combine harvesters and even reaping machines, the corn was cut by hand. First the reaper went through the field cutting armfuls of

corn with a hook. The binder tied the corn into sheaves and stacked the sheaves into piles called stooks. After several days of drying in the sun, the sheaves were loaded onto carts and taken into the barn to be stored. Threshing and winnowing (separating the grain from the chaff) mostly took place during the winter. Gathering in the corn was a long process using all available labour on the farm and often additional casual workers. Bad weather, even for a few days, could be disastrous, spoiling acres of ripe grain and causing poverty and hunger in the months to come. Small wonder, then, that at the end of the harvest, there was huge relief and enormous celebration.

The mystery of the Corn Goddess and the sacrifice of the God remained very real to country people even after Christianity became the main religion. In the Lammas section, we learned of John Barleycorn being the symbol of the God. The Goddess was present in the belief in the Corn Spirit. The Corn Spirit was believed to inhabit the harvest fields and, as the corn was cut, she retreated further and further away from the reapers until she was hiding in the very last sheaf to be cut. It was often called 'the neck' from Celtic words meaning 'saved', because it was eventually kept in the house and not threshed with the rest of the corn. For many years, although this sheaf represented the end of the harvest and was cause for celebration, it was thought unlucky for one man to cut it deliberately. Other means were therefore devised, such as all the reapers throwing their sickles at it so no one single person cut it down. As soon as it was cut it was held up and there were shouts of celebration, such as this one from Devon:

A neck! A neck! A neck!

Who's neck?

Farmer Verris's [or the name of the farmer whose land it was]

It's all a-cut

And all a-bound

And all is taken from the ground!

Hip, hip, hooray!

Then the neck was decorated with ribbons and carried back to the farmyard on a decorated cart pulled by the best oxen or farm horses and then a cry, something like the following, would go up:

We've ploughed, we've sowed,

We've reaped, we've mowed,

We've carried our last load,

And aren't overthrowed!

The sheaf, sometimes made into the shape of a woman, would have pride of place at the harvest supper and would be kept in the farmhouse until the following spring, when it would be ploughed back into the land. Other names for it were the Hare, the Widow and the Kern or Corn Baby and it is not difficult to see how these came about. Sometimes a King and Queen of the Harvest would ride on the cart with the neck and sometimes a young girl, garlanded with flowers.

THINGS TO DO

Song for Mabon

This is a re-write of the traditional song known as 'September' or 'All Among the Barley'.

How swiftly goes September, the Harvest Moon is done,

And over fields of stubble glows the setting sun.

The leaves are turning yellow and fading into red,

While the God of Sun and Harvest is laying down his head.

Gather in the harvest,

Give thanks to the Sun,

For the grain it holds the promise of harvests yet to come.

The Goddess growing older gives grain and fruits and flowers,

She gives us love and nurture to last through winter's hours.

She's Lady of the Harvest, who gives us all she can,
Both now and in the days to come and since the world began.
Gather in the harvest,
Give thanks to the Sun,
For the grain it holds the promise of harvests yet to come.

Dark and light, and day and night, the months of sun and snow,
All are held in balance as the God prepares to go.
The Goddess draws him to her arms as he journeys to the West,
For to wrap him in her love all through the days of sleep and rest.
Gather in the harvest,
Give thanks to the Sun,
For the grain it holds the promise of harvests yet to come.

MEDITATION FOR THE COMPLETED HARVEST

This can be done on any day around Mabon. Read the whole of this through first and remember the main parts of it before you begin. Find a quiet place where you will not be disturbed. Ask the Goddess and God and the Spirits of the Elements to protect you on your inner journey. Take three deep breaths and begin.

Go back to the country lane that you visualised in your Lammas meditation. Notice the changes. The trees are still in full leaf, but already there are yellow leaves among the green. The flowers in the hedgerows are fewer, hawthorn berries and rosehips are bright red. The best blackberries have gone but there are still some to be picked further down the stems. You might see damsons and crab apples. Beyond a hedge you see your harvest field. Walk into it. All the corn has been reaped and piled into stooks on the stubble field. In the centre of the field, on a wooden seat, sits the Goddess, Lady of the Harvest. She is older than when you last saw her but still beautiful. At her feet are bundles of sheaves and a basket of fruits and berries. She smiles and you sit at her feet. She offers you something to drink in a bowl, milk and honey, the

symbols of peace and plenty. You thank her, take it and drink it. Feel her presence and love. Stay there for as long as you wish. When you get up to go, She gives you a sheaf of wheat, telling you that this is your harvest and that you must use it wisely. She gives you the basket of fruits, colourful and glowing in the low autumn Sun. The fruits represent the enrichment that the harvest will bring to your life. There may be another message for you. Only you will know this. Give thanks in your own way and walk back to the lane with joy and gratitude in your heart.

Gradually walk back to the place where you are sitting. Feel the ground under your feet and become aware of the world around you. Open your eyes when you are ready and write down your experiences in your Book of Shadows.

FACING THE DARK

This visualisation can be done on any of the days leading up to Mabon. The light, bright days are behind us and winter's dark is not far away. Like the year, everyone has dark and light aspects to their personalities. No one is wholly good or wholly bad, although most of us would like to think that the balance is more on the good side! Usually everyone has certain aspects about their personality, however small, that even they themselves do not like. Sometimes, it is very hard to admit to them and so they become very hard to put right. The time when we are about to face the dark of winter is also a good time to face these dark aspects of ourselves. Not everybody likes or is ready to do this, so this meditation is not compulsory, but if you feel that you would like to improve something, it can help you to do so. Do not do a large soul-search if it is the first time that you have attempted something like this, but find one or two simple things that will be easy to put right once identified. It takes courage, but you will be really glad and pleased with yourself once your journey is done.

Read the whole of this visualisation through before you begin and memorise as much as you can. However, don't be afraid to improvise or

to let your own imagination add details as you go. These are just guidelines. As usual, find a place to sit where you will not be disturbed. In your head, draw a protective circle of blue light around yourself. Call upon the Spirits of the Elements to protect you on your inner journey. Then call upon the Goddess and God in the following way:

Great Mother, Wise Crone, Lady of the Dark,
I call upon you.
Help me to find the dark secrets of my heart,
That I may put them to rights,
And so better do your service.

Lord of the Shadows, who has no fear of the dark,
I call upon you.
Help me to find the courage to look within,
That I may learn the dark secrets of my heart
And so better walk your ways.

Now think of a pleasant, outdoor place, with some sort of opening into a dark place. This could be a cave by the sea shore, a crack in the rocks, a badger's set, rabbit's hole or fox's den, an opening into a hollow tree, a dark path into a garden or woodland or even a doorway into a friendly feeling house or other building. Take a little time to find the right place for you. Now imagine yourself to be the right size to be able to walk into this opening. Take the first steps inside and come to the beginning of a passageway. Look at your surroundings, feel what is under your feet, become accustomed to them and enjoy them. There is just enough light to see by. Walk along the passageway, taking note of anything that you see on the way. Soon, you come to another doorway or opening and, beyond that, all you can see is velvety black darkness. Stand in the doorway. In the centre of the darkness is a cauldron and the water it contains is shining like silver. On the other side of the cauldron sits a Lady, old and wise, with hooded black cloak. She welcomes you and asks you why you have come.

Tell her that you are searching for the wisdom of the dark. She tells you to look into the cauldron. You sit beside it and stare into it. You may see pictures, you may have feelings, or the Goddess may tell you what you are searching for. You may be surprised or, as often happens, you may learn what you already knew and did not want to admit. Do not be afraid or angry, for the Goddess is there to support you. She understands. She will ask you if you have learned enough for today. Say that you have and thank her in your own way. She tells you that, now you have learned, you will be able to make things right and the opportunity for this will now arise. She bids you go, so you return to the light by the same route, holding your new knowledge within you. When you reach the entrance again, mentally walk back to the place where you are sitting. Feel the real world around you again and open your eyes when you are ready.

In your Book of Shadows, write down your experiences and what you have learned. Take no action now other than accepting the truth. Now you know what is wrong or what should be changed, a solution will probably come very soon.

You have now faced the dark side of yourself and this is an important part of self-knowledge and the inner journey that we travel all our lives. In the future, you will be able to make other journeys and so progress along your own road. Well done.

ASSESSING YOUR HARVEST

At Mabon itself or just before, go back to your Book of Shadows and the drawings of the wheat ears that you made at Lammas. How many more have been cut or are now ready? 'Harvest' them in the same way as before (page 176). Draw them on the next page and garland each one with flowers or with other patterns. Now they are all gathered in, draw a garland or a pattern around all of them together. Underneath, write: 'These are the gifts of the harvest.' Then name or describe the things that you have achieved or learned. Each wheat ear may have brought you more than one gift, or maybe they all contribute to the same thing. Only

you will know this. Write as much or as little as you like. Then write underneath:

My reaping is over, my harvest is in,

One cycle is finished and another begins.

Goddess of Harvest and Lord of the Corn,

I give you my thanks as the year turns.

BIDDING FAREWELL TO THE SUN

You can do this on the night of Mabon itself. The first four lines below, beginning 'Farewell, O Sun…', are from the old Book of Shadows. They are the opening words of the ritual for 'the festival to celebrate the transition of the God from his light aspect to his death aspect' – that is, Mabon or the Autumn Equinox. (The verse is also used in full by Janet and Stewart Farrar in *Eight Sabbats for Witches*).

You will need a brown or orange candle in a cauldron or bowl, and a smaller white one also in a bowl, plus a taper and a candle-snuffer. Work within a cast circle (page 17). Place the brown or orange candle on the western side of the circle and the white candle at the eastern side. Light the taper from one of the altar candles and use it to light the brown candle. If possible, keep the taper burning. One person says:

The Sun is journeying towards the West

And soon our days will be dark.

The brown candle is put out. The same person or someone else says:

Farewell, O Sun, ever returning Light,

The Hidden God, who ever yet remains,

Who now departs to the Lands of Youth,

Through the Gates of Death.

The same voice or another voice continues:

As we go forward in our lives,

We go back into the dark.

Each step towards enlightenment
Is a step towards the ultimate end,
Which is not an end,
But another beginning.
For, like the Sun after the dark days [The white candle is quickly
lit here], we will all be reborn.

Then dance the spiral dance as for Litha (page 156), the only difference being that this time you spiral anticlockwise into the centre, which represents going into the dark, and spiral out clockwise. The song, chant or tune given for Litha can also be used here, but miss out the lines beginning 'The Wheel of the Year turns'. Ground the energy in the same way as described for Litha.

THE LESSON OF THE GRAIN

The grain and the harvest can teach us many things. These are the essence of the festival. Try this ritual on the night of Mabon itself.

You will need either one ear of wheat placed in the centre of a plate or dish, or three or four wheat ears together with two dried poppy seedheads, tied with green ribbon. You will also need a thin or empty wheat ear or something to represent famine, plus a piece of bread, an incense stick in a holder, some cinnamon oil and a small glass of wine. Finally you will need a bowl of broken-up dried stalks, either of wheat or of any garden herbs, such as fennel, that have gone to seed, plus a small paper bag. Work within a cast circle (page 17).

The ritual works for a single person or a group. Simply change the words to fit. The words 'Behold the mystery...' come from the Eleusinian mysteries of ancient Greece and are quoted by Janet and Stewart Farrar in *Eight Sabbats for Witches*. They are very appropriate here and can help you to concentrate.

The group stands in a circle, with a single person standing in the centre. One person says:

The harvest is completed,

The grain of the spring's sowing gathered in. [The wheat is placed in the centre of the circle.]

Behold the mystery. In silence is the seed of wisdom gained.

Let us reflect upon our own harvest.

Have we reaped with gladness

The ripened grain of our own setting?

Did our ideas come to fruition?

Were the tasks we set ourselves completed?

We reflect on the year's successes.

Not the material successes of money made or contracts won,

But the inner tasks that only ourselves shall know.

The lessons learned,

The knowledge gained,

The fears overcome,

The attitude changed,

The vista shifted,

The bridges built,

The small but startling steps towards self-knowledge.

All these are our summer's harvest,

The food of our spirituality.

Every step forward,

Every grain reaped,

Brings us nearer to the God and Goddess within.

Everyone says or sings the chorus:

Gather in the harvest,

Give thanks to the Sun,

For the grain it holds the promise of harvests yet to come.

Another voice can take over here if wished:

We give thanks to the Goddess and God for our own harvest.

We pledge to use it wisely.

It will sustain us through the time of rest.

It holds the seeds to be planted in the spring

To set us off on new journeys,

New beginnings.

Every lesson or realisation is a harvest of grain.

As the grain holds the seeds of new life,

So every lesson learned

Brings us to a new task.

We learn a lesson,

Which gives us new skills,

Which can be practised

To learn another lesson.

As the harvest and the planting,

So our endings and beginnings.

This is the lesson of the harvest.

We celebrate the grain, the fruits,

And the Earth's abundance.

[The wheat is held up.]

We gain our wisdom from the seed.

All say or sing:

Gather in the harvest,

Give thanks to the Sun,

For the grain it holds the promise of harvests yet to come.

The empty wheat ear or other representation of famine is put into the centre. One person says:

Where one person reaps plenty,

Another may have famine.

May we who have plenty

Learn to share.

One person takes the piece of bread to the North and says:

> May we be willing to share our wealth and our food that all the people in the world may be free from starvation and poverty.

One person takes the incense to the East and says:

> May we give freely of our ideas and thoughts, so that wisdom may be shared for the good of all.

One person takes the cinnamon oil to the South, rubs a small amount on the South candle and says:

> May we share our passion and courage to bring warmth and enthusiasm into the lives of others.

One person takes the wine to the West and says:

> May we share the positive emotions of love, sympathy and happiness, and strive to banish hatred and sorrow from the world.

The first voice says:

> May these things that we share work together to bring about peace and co-operation between all the people of the world, regardless of race, religion, age, ability, status or sexual orientation, or any other differences that there may be between us. [The 'famine' is taken away and the bowl of stalks put into the centre of the circle.]
> We now look once more at our own harvest.
> When the harvest is gathered in
> We keep the seed and throw away the stalks.
> We take the unwanted parts of our harvest
> And throw them away without guilt or regret.

Everyone then thinks about the parts of the year's projects that are no longer relevant to their lives and mentally projects them onto the stalks

in the bowl. After a pause, tip the contents of the bowl into the paper bag and the same voice continues:

    These we will scatter to the four winds,

    So they bring no harm to anything on Earth.

Seal the top of the bag and, as soon as possible, scatter the stalks somewhere outside, saying:

    Winds of North and South and East and West,

    Blow these stalks so they come to rest

    Scattered for ever on the Earth's floor

    And never come to trouble us more.

GIVING THANKS AND HEALING TO THE EARTH AND THE ELEMENTS

This is a way of acknowledging the gifts of the harvest, giving thanks and sharing or putting something back. Work within a cast circle, either singly or with others. You will need a single wheat ear or small bunch of wheat, a stone, a small bowl or clear bottle of water, a small twig bearing green leaves, a feather and a round object such as a crystal, or even a large marble, to be a symbol of the Earth.

Put the grain into the centre of the circle. One person says:

    The Earth has given us the harvest of grain,

    The Goddess and God have fulfilled our inner dreams,

    The Elements of our life have worked in harmony,

    We have reaped joy and sorrow, achievements and lessons.

    For all of this,

    And for all of our lives,

    We give thanks.

Another or the same person says:

    We hold in our hands the fruit of our harvest.

Our hands are full, there is plenty to share.

In thanks we will work to heal the Earth

Her sacred places, her waters, her forests, her air.

[A stone is put into the centre.]

May her sacred places be ever protected.

[A small bowl or bottle of water put into the centre.]

May her waters flow clear on every shore.

[A twig is put into the centre.]

May we safeguard her forests and woodland places,

[A feather is put into the centre.]

May the air that she breathes be made clean and pure.

[The Earth symbol is put into the centre.]

May we all work to make this come to be,

In any way that each one of us knows,

So that every small space on the Earth that is cared for,

Joins up worldwide and continues to grow.

All sing or say:

Gather in the harvest,

Give thanks to the Sun,

For the grain it holds the promise of harvests yet to come.

HARVEST HOME

Working traditional rhymes and customs into your own rituals gives you a feeling of continuity and of being in touch with the Earth in a way that our ancestors were, whatever their religion. Add a few words or change a few words and you have something that is relevant to your life now. Use the Mary Barleycorn that you made for Lammas (page 180) or make one specially now. Everyone present will need a small piece of ribbon, or brightly coloured cord or embroidery thread with a bead on the end (the kind that are used for hair wraps) or any other type of small decoration that can be easily tied. Work within a cast

circle (page 17). While Mary Barleycorn is being passed around the circle, everyone should bear in mind their own personal harvest.

One person holds up Mary Barleycorn and says:

It's all a-cut and all a-bound,

And all is taken from the ground.

Then pass the Mary Barleycorn clockwise around the circle for each person to tie on a small decoration, saying, at the same time:

My harvest is gathered,

My year's work done,

I give thanks to God and Goddess for Harvest Home.

Mary Barleycorn is taken to the centre again and held up. Everyone says:

We've ploughed, we've sowed,

We've reaped, we've mowed,

We are all one more step along the road.

Blessed be.

If there are quite a lot of people in your circle, you may find it easier for one person simply to tie one large ribbon around Mary Barleycorn, such as a sash around her waist. They then say the words on behalf of everybody, beginning 'Our harvest' instead of 'My'.

MABON INCENSE

1 teaspoon frankincense

1 teaspoon myrrh

1 teaspoon juniper berries, crushed

1 teaspoon dried marigold petals

½ teaspoon dried sage

2 drops benzoin oil

2 drops cinnamon oil

Have a brown or maroon coloured cloth and candles and use ears of wheat and autumn berries for decorations. Place seed heads of herbs in a vase with dried lavender sprigs. Brown coloured chrysanthemums are also suitable.

CAKES AND WINE

In the Celtic tree calendar, late September is the Vine Month so a drink made from grapes is appropriate. A warming, dark brown sherry seems just the thing for Mabon. Mix it with grape juice for a lighter flavour. Years ago, when I first started writing cookery books, a local Kent person sent me a recipe called 'Oastcakes to eat at a Hopkin'. A Hopkin is the celebration that takes place in the oast house (where hops are dried) when all the hops (that are used to flavour beer) are gathered in. As this is a harvest celebration, I have used it here. It first appeared in my book *Country Wisdom*, long since out of print.

Spiced sherry cup

8fl oz/225ml medium sherry

16fl oz/450ml white grape juice

2 cinnamon sticks

Mix the sherry and grape juice in a jug and put in the cinnamon sticks. Cover and leave at room temperature for around eight hours. Remove the cinnamon sticks before serving.

Oastcakes to eat at a Hopkin

4oz/125g wholemeal flour

4oz/125g plain white flour

pinch salt

1 teaspoon baking powder

2oz/50g lard or butter

2oz/50g currants

4 tablespoons water

approximately 7fl oz/200ml white wine (the original was parsnip wine)

sunflower oil for frying

Put the flour, salt and baking powder into a bowl. Rub in half the lard and mix in the currants. Beat in the water and enough wine to make a very soft, batter-like dough. Heat the remaining butter or lard in the frying pan and add oil to the depth of 6mm. Drop in tablespoons of the dough, spread them out and fry them until they are golden on both sides. They are best eaten straight away, but if you are going to use them in the circle, cut them into small pieces and put them on a plate. Cover them with foil and keep them warm in a low oven. Bring them into the circle covered in the foil and uncover them just before you need them.

The complete Mabon ritual

Cast your circle (page 17), then invoke the Goddess and God in the following way:

> We call upon you, Great Mother of us all,
> By seed and root,
> By shoot and stem,
> By stalk and leaf and grain,
> We call upon you now
> To descend upon us,
> That we may accept your gift of harvest,
> And learn its lessons,
> So that within us your service may be fulfilled.

> Lord of the Harvest,
> Of life and death,
> Light and dark,
> Summer and winter,

We call upon you now,

As you turn to the Shadowlands,

To descend upon us,

So that we may walk forever in your ways.

Then use the ideas suggested earlier in this chapter to cover all the following activities:

- Song for Mabon: if you are working in a group, have individuals sing or say the verses and everyone join in the refrain, 'Gather in the harvest...' etc. The refrain is used in other parts of the ritual, joining it together.
- Bidding farewell to the Sun, with the spiral dance at the end
- The lesson of the grain
- Giving thanks and healing to the Earth and the Elements
- Harvest home
- Cakes and wine.

Blessing

Mabon is:

Spider webs and dewy mornings,

Loaded apple trees,

Rooks flying home,

Turning leaves and shortening days,

The storing of the grain and Harvest Home.

May we all accept the harvest gifts of the Goddess and God with thanks and love and gladness. May we use them for the good of the world, for the good of others and of ourselves. May we keep them and nurture them through the winter, to plant seeds of joy and love in the coming spring. Blessed be.

Close the circle.

CHAPTER 9

THE WAY FORWARD

Read more books about the Wiccan way. Keep celebrating the festivals, setting yourself projects of self-development and writing in your Book of Shadows. Put your own words into the seasonal rituals. Learn about full Moons and rites of passage. Take up new skills of healing or divination. Go out and find traditional calendar customs, both from your own tradition and from those of other races and creeds. Do not boast about your chosen pathway or criticise other people's religions and beliefs and do not set out actively to convert people. If people ask you about your way of life, try to answer them clearly and honestly.

Enjoy the turning Wheel of the Wiccan year and let it enrich your life and the lives of others.

Blessed be.

RESOURCES

STARCHILD

The Courtyard,

2–4, High Street,

Glastonbury,

Somerset,

BA6 9DU

01458 834663

Suppliers of dried herbs, spices, gums and resins; essential oils, burning oils, a wide variety of incense blends, candles, charcoal and much more. Mail order catalogue available.

G BALDWIN AND CO

171–173, Walworth Road,

London,

SE1 1RW

020 7703 5550

Suppliers of dried herbs, spices, gums, resins, essential oils, oil burners, base oils, small selection of prepared incense, plus other things like soap and vitamins. Mail order catalogue available.